LANDSCAPE OF PRAYER
Murray Bodo

ST. ANTHONY MESSENGER PRESS
Cincinnati, Ohio

Scripture citations are taken from the *New Revised Standard Version Bible,* copyright ©1989 by the Division of Christian Education of the National Council of Churches of Christ in the U.S.A. and used by permission.

"Holy Orders: An Inner Album" first appeared as "Holy Orders" in *Signatures of Grace: Catholic Writers on the Sacraments* (E. P. Dutton, 2000); "At Merton's Hermitage" first appeared in *Image: A Journal of the Arts and Religion*; "The Evergreen Tree: Praying with the Dalai Lama" first appeared in a slightly altered version in *St. Anthony Messenger* magazine.

Cover and book design by Mark Sullivan

Library of Congress Cataloging-in-Publication Data

Bodo, Murray.
  Landscape of prayer / Murray Bodo.
    p. cm.
  ISBN 0-86716-517-0 (pbk.)
  1. Prayer—Catholic Church. 2. Contemplation. 3. Bodo, Murray. I. Title.
  BV210.3.B63 2003
  248.3'2--dc21

                                    2002155146

ISBN 0-86716-517-0

Published by St. Anthony Messenger Press
www.AmericanCatholic.org
Printed in the U.S.A.

To Jeremy Harrington, O.F.M.,
editor, publisher, mentor—
for thirty years of encouragement
in good times and bad.

Contents

Acknowledgments

I wish to thank all those whose generosity and kindness contributed to the writing of this book. All those whose homes and hospitality provided prayer-and-writing space along the way: Susan Saint Sing, Deborah Gaffaney, Doug Shannon, Andy and Mildred Piano, Brother Giles Kelly at the Franciscan Retreat House on Cape Cod, Sister Jeanette Serra and the Edmundite Community at Enders Island, Brother Jon Bankert and the Episcopal Franciscan Community at Little Portion Friary, Long Island; Brother Gerald Grantner and the Franciscan Friars at St. Michaels, Arizona; Don Aldo Brunacci and *la famiglia* at Casa Papa Giovanni in Assisi. A man named Bill, who made it possible for me to fly-fish the stream at Tamarack. Those whose suggestions and corrections helped to improve the text: Franciscan Friars, Jack Wintz, Thomas Richstatter and Gerald Grantner; Pat Mora, Erin McGraw, Susan Saint Sing, Mari Messer, Chris Jordan; and my editor, April Bolton.

PART ONE:
Sitting in the Mystery

In the Image of God

Prayer is taking time to go apart and talk with God. The place apart need not be a dwelling. It can even be a place inside yourself. It can be a spot in nature like the sand hill across from my boyhood home where I would often sit nights and look at the stars. It was my sacred place of wonder and contemplation. I would leave home, cross the dirt road and climb the hill.

In the years since, those simple gestures of leaving, crossing and climbing have become increasingly important to me as defining outer and inner movements in the landscape of prayer. Sometimes, paradoxically, climbing is actually descending. The descent-as-ascent gesture is, for example, contained in Christ's admonitions, "all who humble themselves will be exalted" (Matthew 23:12) and "those who lose their life for my sake will find it" (Matthew 16:25). The gesture of descending that is a rising is, of course, the very gesture Christ's own life makes,

> who, though he was in the form of God,
> did not regard equality with God
> as something to be exploited,
> but emptied himself,
> taking the form of a slave,
> being born in human likeness. . . . (Philippians 2:6–8)

Jesus, the Son of God, descends from the Father, makes the crossing to dwell among us, away from his homeland. And when he prays, he goes apart in order to commune with the Father, to remember where he came from and where he will ascend again. We, too, have come from God and need to go aside to remember where we've come from and where we are returning.

Unfortunately, the gestures our lives make tend to be circular and narcissistic, so that it takes a real effort to break out of the circle of self, to cross over the dirt road, and ascend or descend to some place of remembering who we really are. That simple journey constitutes all myth. And prayer involves the stuff of myth, a personal myth experienced in that profound gesture Martin Buber described as moving from an I-It to an I-Thou relationship. Prayer is the internalizing of an I-Thou relationship with God, which had become an I-It relationship (something outside my personal relating) through the circular gesture of the self turned in upon itself.

Though prayer may *begin* with a heightened awareness of the self, its ultimate gesture is a breaking out of self-absorption and moving to the Other. Paradoxically, this crossing over to the Other, this breaking through and out of the narcissistic self, is marked by an awareness that the Other has broken through to me. Prayer is not so much what I do, therefore, as it is taking the time to go apart from self-absorption long enough to experience what God is doing in me.

I leave home and cross the dirt road to climb the hill and look at the stars that were there all along apart from my seeing. When I look at them with this new vision, my whole life becomes starstruck, as it were. Thus it is in prayer: we make those gestures that enable us to see what was there all along, the image of God, who is Creator, Redeemer and Sanctifier, imprinted on our very soul. That image contemplated will enable us to know who we really are. We experience the truth about ourselves in prayer, but then we begin to forget as we descend the hill and cross the road to our ordinary lives again. And so we have to keep making the journey back to the symbolic sand hill; we return lest the image within begins to fade and we find ourselves going around in circles once more, locked onto a false image of who we are. We know we've forgotten God's image when we begin to refuse gestures of "crossing over"—gestures like reaching out to others less fortunate, gestures of prayer that are more than self-absorbed whines, gestures of contemplation of the other, from a flower, to a human being, to God.

When I realize my gestures are really movements of self-embracing that don't simultaneously embrace God and all God's creation, then I know it's time to enter prayer again. For the image of God in me is one of a God who reaches out from an intense, inner trinitarian life to create the universe. This trinitarian image in me, the more intensely and intimately I contemplate it, moves me to move out of my own self-absorbed love to creative gestures of love outside myself, *ad extra*, as medieval theologians put it.

The home we leave when we enter into prayer is ultimately the home of the self turned in upon itself. The hill of contemplation allows us to look on the same self as an image of its trinitarian Creator. We go apart to see what is already there. And that act of seeing, of contemplation, moves us to gestures like those of the Creator whose image we see in our own soul. We find our self when we lose self-absorption in contemplation of the image of the Creator.

A threefold image that is one: Creator, Redeemer, Sanctifier. The one image of who I am is the result of a threefold gesture of the one God who creates me, redeems me, sanctifies me. In prayer I realize that every authentic gesture (within and without) on my part is a response of gratitude for the threefold gesture of God within me. And in order to maintain that authenticity over a lifetime, I need to enter prayer again and again in order to contemplate the image of God that I am, an image that fades into false images which my daily life seems inevitably to substitute for the true image.

Sitting in the Mystery

I am sitting in an easy chair, one of my mother's sixty-year-old Navajo rugs at my feet. The smell of its wool, the red, black and brown patterns summon up images of my mother shaking out this and other Navajo rugs on mornings after the numerous March sandstorms that worried her cleaning every year in our rented house in Gallup, New Mexico—the last in a series of mining towns we lived in when I was a boy.

This morning I said Sunday Mass at a small table in a makeshift hermitage—a borrowed house of a couple on vacation—my mother's rug spread again at my feet. Her presence is woven into the pattern of my life—her words remembered, her ever-busy hands stirring polenta, making beds, removing ashes from the coal cooking stove and the living room heating stove, her hands turning the pages of the books she read to me— *Huckleberry Finn*, most memorably—she, whose formal education never went beyond the eighth grade, but who loved to read. I see her behind the beard reflected in the mirror where I shave and comb my hair.

I sit here in the mystery of the life we all live and try to understand, knowing at this time in my life that everything is gift to be celebrated and returned to God in praise. Why I am the son of this mother is gift, is mystery. Why she seems so alive here beside me is mystery—her voice almost audible, her hand almost guiding my pen as I write. Almost. For, like all those we turn to for guidance, for answers, for wisdom to live by, for assurance that this present existence is not all there is, my mother is just beyond my reach.

A "V" of geese flies by my window. I see them but can't fly with them, can't become them. They are wings I long for but I must sit instead in the mystery of my own and their otherness. The geese, my mother and I, like the threads of this rug at my feet are a part of the pattern seen only by another, the Other, the God, who is both outside and within the pattern we all make together and individually.

The daily prayer I enter here in this chair, this rug at my feet, is simply sitting in the mystery of the interwoven meaning we make together. At times if I take the time to sit here, I almost see into the mystery. Almost. For, like my departed mother's presence in this rug, I can almost touch it, but not quite. Touch "it." The only word I can use for the mystery is "it." "It" is indefinable, indescribable, yet draws me to return to this chair and rug for the almost-touch which assures me, consoles me with the presence of something beyond, trying to reach me as I, in turn, try to reach out to it. In this reciprocal reaching, almost touching, is the mystery of my daily prayer.

I come to this place, a corner of whatever room the rug rests in, because I need the almost-touch of mystery. We all do. For that which is tangible, seeable, that which we can hear and taste, that which we can define, measure, possess or understand or control, does not satisfy and only reminds us of its mortality, its diminishing and passing away. Mystery invites us into eternity, that meeting of what we now experience as almost-touches—a meeting that is effected by a passage through death. Sitting in the mystery reminds us that death *is* a passage which removes the "almost" from that daily reaching out to touch what reaches out to touch us beyond our knowing and seeing.

Absolute Poverty

The TV screen statics into a late-breaking news report. TWA Flight 800, bound for Paris, has crashed shortly after taking off from New York's Kennedy Airport. It is reported to have exploded in the sky over Long Island Sound. . . . A group of Olympic fans, gathered for a late night concert in downtown Atlanta's Olympic Park, suddenly experience a loud report, a rush of air and flying debris. Two people die and over a hundred are injured. . . . Columbine High School: the horror of children killing children. . . . The American psyche reels. These incidents, like the bombing of an American military residence in Saudi Arabia, the bombing of the Federal Building in Oklahoma City, the bombing of the World Trade Center in New York City and, most dramatically, the attack on the twin towers of the World Trade Center, their collapse and the loss of thousands of lives, the attack on the Pentagon, the anthrax scare, further expose the illusion that America is a safe haven from the violence and terrorism that threatens the rest of the world. Fear and anger and anxiety grip America's soul.

What, we ask, is happening? Where are we headed? Is there nowhere to turn for peace of mind? Instinctively, we know there is no escape, and even if there were, escape is not a solution. Here, as always, we must turn and face our demons, find a way to exorcize them, redeem their pernicious effect on our lives. And though we cannot, will not, escape, we relearn the wisdom of prayer as recouping, reenergizing, renewing the sources of courage and peace and genuine love. We turn inward, reach down deep within for the center, that source of integration, the self that cannot be blown apart by bombs or hatred or death.

The Trappist monk Thomas Merton wrote of this deep center in *Conjectures of a Guilty Bystander*:

> At the center of our being is a point of nothingness
> which is untouched by sin and by illusion, a point of
> pure truth, a point or spark which belongs entirely

to God, which is never at our disposal, from which God disposes of our lives, which is inaccessible to the fantasies of our own mind or the brutalities of our own will. This little point of nothingness and of absolute poverty is the pure glory of God in us. It is so to speak his name written in us, as our poverty, as our indigence, as our dependence, as our sonship. It is like a pure diamond, blazing with the invisible light of heaven. It is in everybody, and if we could see it we would see these billions of points of light coming together in the dance and blaze of the sun that would make all the darkness and cruelty of life vanish completely. I have no program for this seeing. It is only given. But the gate of heaven is everywhere.[1]

As I begin to reflect upon this center from my own Franciscan perspective, these words of Saint Francis to his brothers rise like a gift from my own center,

Wherever we are or wherever we are going, we have our cell with us. For Brother Body is the cell, and the soul is the hermit who dwells in it, meditating and praying to God. Therefore, if the soul does not preserve quiet and solitude in its own cell, of what profit is a cell made of hands?[2]

These words in turn reminded me of other words spoken by the Venerable Maha Ghosananda, the "Ghandi of Cambodia," in a retreat at Gethsemani Abbey in Kentucky.

We Buddhists must find the courage to leave our temples and enter the temples of human experience, temples that are filled with suffering. If we listen to the Buddha, Christ or Ghandi, we can do nothing else. The refugee camps, the prisons, the ghettos and the battlefields will then become our temples. . . . Many Cambodians tell me, "Venerable monks belong in the temple." It is difficult for them to adjust to this new role, but we monks must answer the increasingly loud cries of suffering. We only need to remember that our temple is with us always. We *are* our temple.

And earlier this same summer a Navajo medicine man told me of his grandfather's words, "A Navajo doesn't have to worry about leaving the reservation, because wherever he goes, he carries his mountains with him."

Cell, temple, mountains. Words that summon up other words: inner room, tent, ascent. A further trinity of words that symbolize the soul, itself a trinitarian unity of mind, will and emotions.

To pray is to journey inward and refind our soul. We may travel outward to facilitate this inner journey, but it is the inner journey that is the prayer, an inner journey that involves an ascent of a high mountain where there is a sacred tent that one enters in order to descend to another inner room. And this inner journey can be made anywhere, from a monastery to a seat in an airplane, to a hotel room at the Olympic Games.

The inner journey is not unlike writing itself. The very words above began on the back porch, with the early morning sun streaking the grass and making sparkle the beads of water on the leaves of the redbud and dogwood trees surrounding me. The words found their rounding, their completion in a gray chair in the lobby of the Pain Control Clinic at Christ Hospital in Cincinnati, where I waited for someone who was undergoing steroid treatment for chronic pain. There were people seated, talking around me. The sound of their talking dissolved in the air of my pen scratching out its own words on the page.

The writing became a kind of prayer, an inner journey made in circumstances some would claim unsuited for writing. But writing, like journeying inward, happens when we are doing it. *Where* we are doing the writing or praying is not as important as the actual *doing* itself. As one spiritual master remarked, "Stay with your prayer-practice and the practice will bring you where you want to be, no matter where you are when you meditate."

And thus I have entered into God. I've found a place within where I can face the terrible tragedies that drove me inward. I have found a place of peace from which I'll emerge God-centered in my responses to whatever tragedy life brings. God will direct my way from the deep center, the place of absolute poverty within.

Notes

[1] Thomas Merton, *Conjectures of a Guilty Bystander* (New York: Doubleday and Co., 1966), p. 71.

[2] *Legend of Perugia*, 80. See *Omnibus of the Sources for the Life of St. Francis of Assisi,* Marion A. Habig, ed. (Chicago: Franciscan Herald Press, 1972), p. 1056. Cf. Murray Bodo, *Through the Year with Francis of Assisi* (Cincinnati: St. Anthony Messenger Press, 1993), p. 85.

Learning to Listen

How anxious and insecure modern life has made us all. There is no security in jobs, in previously sacred and enduring relationships like marriage and family. Financial planning and health insurance seem preempted by others who often are motivated more by profit than by our welfare. Basic values that hold a society together threaten to collapse. Corporate takeovers and euphemisms like "downsizing" continue to justify cruel and inhuman consequences in people's lives. Simulation and appearance are given such priority that we appropriate and replicate, neglecting our own potential for creativity and generativity.

In such a milieu prayer is the search for authenticity, identity and security that transcends and exposes all false securities (like certain stocks and bonds of the same name). Prayer is a return to listening (the word *authenticity* derives from the Latin, *audire*, "to hear"), a return to the soul, from which all identity derives, a return to God, who is the source of everything, the One in whom all mere appearance and falsehood are exposed. We come to prayer, then, to learn to listen, to find our soul, to find God (who is the One we listen to in the depths of our soul).

The process of listening is something even the so-called non-religious person submits to in order to get beyond the noise that constantly assaults our hearing. In an interview for *Intuition* magazine, the novelist Isabel Allende says of her own creative process,

> I try to separate myself from the noise. Life is noise. In order to hear those voices and to understand the stories that are floating, I need silence. That silence is not something that I can get easily. I am not only thinking of the silence without the phone ringing, I am talking about the silence in my head that the writing requires. For that, I have developed certain tiny rituals; for example, I light a candle at my desk and I have a photograph of my daughter, my grandmother and

my mother. These are the feminine spirits that inspire
me and help and protect me. . . . I light a candle and I
ask them to be with me. I spend a few minutes in total
silence trying to empty my head.[1]

As soon as I copied these words of Isabel Allende into my notebook, I lit a candle before the pictures of my mother and father
that I keep on my desk, I said a brief prayer, I spent a few minutes in silence. Out of this small ritual came these words, "What
is the place within where I can listen, find my soul, meet God?"
And that brief question moved the words I've been writing to
something personal. I became aware of my own evasions, my own
borrowings and lack of authenticity. I realized how much trust I
put in false securities. I knew I had to refind my own sacred
space within.

That is what ritual, prayer and silence do. They center us and
move us beyond the vacuous thoughts that rattle noisily in our
heads. They summon us to take responsibility for our own lives.
They move us from heard to heart.

In the same interview Allende says of the writing she had
done the day before,

I sat down and I started writing something with the
feeling that my heart wasn't there, that it was a good
story, probably a very commercial book, but I wasn't
connected to the story. So last night I had a strange
feeling that I had not really done anything. I woke up
suddenly in the middle of the night with the need to
write something else. I started writing something like
a letter to my agent that I knew I would never send,
but I had the freedom to write what I really wanted to
write. I started something quite different, and most
probably that is going to be the book. . . .[2]

What Allende says here of writing is analogous to what happens
in prayer. We go in a rather cerebral search for God and the self;
we are determined to listen and understand. Then, in entering
the silence, something unanticipated happens: we find our heart
of hearts, and it has its own agenda.

NOTES

[1] *Intuition*, May/June 1996, p. 26.
[2] Ibid., p. 26.

Ways into the Soul

Were we to hear God speak, we would have no need of faith, for we would have knowledge, certainty. And so we, like the ancients, have faith in that which is unseen, unheard. We believe on the testimony of others, those chosen few who have heard God speak. As Christians we believe, most of all, the witness of Jesus, who is the Word of God made flesh. Jesus is the Way, the Truth and the Life, the Word of God that every human being can hear. He came among us as one of us, his gestures showing us how we are to live. He spoke, and his words are spirit and life.

To live out the words of Jesus is to live in faith, for they can only be lived in faith. And so we are back to the original problem. God speaks to the ancients, God speaks through the prophets, and ultimately in and through Jesus—all historical figures no longer walking among us—and we believe because of the words others have left us of what these graced souls said and did. Is that all we're left with? Or does God in fact speak to the modern soul, as well? Can I in prayer find a place of hearing where God speaks to me?

The wisdom of the ages says there is such a place, and it is within. And what is more, if we enter there, God will "open our deafness," as Saint Augustine says so beautifully. The speaking is God's, the entering into the place of hearing is ours.

How is it, then, that I enter there? There are different ways in. I will name a few. One way is to enter by means of a word. I find my word, as it were, the word that disposes me most to prayerful listening. Sometimes I choose a word, at other times a word is given to me. For example, the word that most disposes me to prayer and leads me into that place of hearing is "Jesus." "Jesus," repeated over and over again, the word itself becoming more internal as my recitation moves from a whisper to an inner echo. In that word is everything I know and desire and, like the word "Beatrice" for Dante, it works a transformation of my whole being. Just as the name "Beatrice" beckoned Dante to a higher, selfless love, so the name "Jesus" beckons me to Love itself.

In carrying the name "Jesus" into the inner place of hearing, I begin to hear the words Jesus spoke in the Gospels; I begin to see Jesus healing the sick, feeding the hungry, calming the storm, dying on the cross, rising from the dead. And all these images, impressed on my soul, become "words" of God sounding in the inner ear. What before was exterior, in the printed words of a book or in the voice of a preacher, is now heard inside where the soul receives the words and stores them for drawing upon in times of barrenness and trial. "[S]tore up for yourselves treasure in heaven," Jesus says, "where neither moth nor rust consumes" (Matthew 6:20). Prayer does just that. It stores up treasure in the heaven within, in the soul.

Another way in is simply through silence and the desire for God to be revealed. The desire for God's personal revelation implies openness to whatever God may say, openness to however the revelation may happen. One way to wait in the silence of desire is to remember how God touched your life in the past. Beginning with childhood you begin to see and give thanks for the images that spontaneously rise into your consciousness. Images that elicit a "Yes, God was there. I kiss the hand of God that delivered me, consoled me, challenged me or simply made me aware that God was there for me."

At the time it may have seemed that God had abandoned you, God was far from you; and now you see by hindsight that what you experienced as an abandonment by God was really God leading you in a direction you did not want to go, or it could be that God did indeed veil God's face, so that you had to draw on the deepest sources of faith within you.

This inventory of God-images from the past disposes you to be open to whatever intimacy God is offering you here and now. Openness is all. Even openness to the non-revelation of God. For God's arm cannot be twisted, so to speak; God's revelation is gift, and only in waiting will that gift be given. Waiting in silence and listening.

An image that defines my own deepest desire for God was given me in a few lines from *Winnie the Pooh.*

Piglet sidled up to Pooh from behind.

"Pooh!" he whispered.

"Yes, Piglet?"

"Nothing," said Piglet, taking Pooh's paw. "I just wanted to be sure of you."

I don't know exactly where the quote comes from; it was sent to me as a greeting card. I accepted it as coming from God, because at that very time I was struggling with how to express what I want from God, who I want God to be for me. And there it was in that little scene, that brief dialogue.

To me the desire of every prayer is to somehow be sure God is there. The whole of one's praying is a way of sidling up to God and whispering, "God!" The fear is that there will be no, "Yes?" And often there is not. But as in other disciplines persevered in, the discipline of prayer, of silent longing, does facilitate a receptivity to what in the end is pure gift—God's "Yes?"

A History of Prayer

cঙ্গ৯

Words and Books

I t begins with rote learning, those formulas we can rattle off because we learned them in childhood the way we learned the alphabet or the Pledge of Allegiance. They stick with us, those learned prayers, though often we can't remember where or when we learned them. At least, I can't remember that time—it was sometime before I was five years old because that's when I entered kindergarten in Sacred Heart School in Gallup, New Mexico. And by then I knew my prayers.

From confidence in knowing our prayers, we graduate to the guilt imposed on us if we fail to "say our prayers." Guilt and fear. Now we move imperceptively from limbo, that nowhere between sin and virtue, to purgatory itself, that somewhere where we atone through patient suffering for our sins precipitated, we are told, because we failed to say our prayers. And that's the way it begins, prayer as compulsive recitation of formulas that must be said just as we learned them, word by word. And we are thereby locked into a curious dilemma; if we don't say our prayers the way we learned them, we're somehow sinning; and yet there are movements of the heart that beckon us to spontaneity, to conversing with God the way we would talk with someone we love and trust. But fear restrains us. What if talking with God spontaneously is too familiar? What if words other than those Jesus taught us in the Our Father don't work and God won't hear? And so we remain on fear's plateau until something happens to shake us into the truth which is a step beyond formulaic prayers.

This step beyond began for me when I began reading Thomas Merton between customers in Dad's Gallup Sporting Goods store, when I was thirteen. The book was Merton's first autobiography, *The Seven Storey Mountain* (first, because in one sense almost everything he wrote was autobiography).

The way Merton talked about prayer, the way he prayed right there on the page, engaged me as few books had before then. His words were seductive. They drew me into a world I longed to enter, a world of seemingly continuous, familiar discourse with God. Merton had the key, I was sure, to how to open the doors of heaven. I knew little of prayer then and how much of it is gift: God's initiative, God's working in us, God's choosing or not choosing to reveal the Divine Presence.

I was young and inexperienced yet, but determined to pray the way the saints prayed, the way Merton's beautiful words outlined praying as a way of living. Merton's words were reinforced when I entered the high school seminary the following year and made my first retreat. I wasn't sure what it was all about, and today, over fifty years and many retreats later, I'm still not sure what it is that moves the heart to enter silence and solitude and sacred space. Nor am I sure I know all that happens there in that place removed, yet at the center of who I am.

I'm not sure because that which moves the heart is as various and complex and yet as simple as the human heart itself. Saint Augustine says in his *Confessions*, "Our hearts, O God, are made for thee, and they cannot rest until they rest in thee." Is that why we enter into prayer? Surely, that is a major reason, but to say that Augustine's words alone, and no others, are the motivation for entering into prayer is to turn simplicity into simplification. It is to over-simplify, to reduce to definition, what in the end partakes more of mystery and of the divine than of human classification and simple explanation.

When I made my first retreat, I did so because I was told to do so. It was what a young seminarian did as part of his spiritual growth. You were freed from classes for four or five days. You went into chapel and listened to retreat talks by a visiting priest, you tried to keep silence and to pray more, to kneel before the altar of Mary and the various saints whose altars lined the walls on each side of the chapel. You read spiritual books like *The Imitation of Christ* and the lives of the saints. There was no radio blaring in the recreation room, no tick and click of Ping-Pong or pool balls. There were long walks in the woods. The school quieted down. Then, when the retreat ended, the noise level rose, classes resumed, adolescent competition and inner turmoil continued.

Did something happen in those few days of retreat? If so, did it last and how is it manifest in my life today? If in no other way, those early retreats made each year of high school seminary help me to recognize retreat-like experiences in my life today. For example, I am training west on Amtrak's Southwest Chief as I write these words. I am in an economy sleeper. The door is closed, the atmosphere prayerful. It feels a lot like one of those seminary retreats when I was a teenager. I leave the world of phones and doorbells. I travel a pair of rails monotonously but rhythmically back to my roots, to Gallup where I was born. I enter the cave of my sleeping compartment as into a kind of moving retreat.

What is happening here I remember happening when I was fourteen years old. I feel uncomfortable at first. I'm leaving loved ones behind. But what will I do to fill up the time? Should I hang around the club car? Look for someone to be near? Stay in my sleeper and pray, read, meditate? Will the silence scare me? What if I'm more tempted now that there is no TV, sports, people, work, obligations, schedule, to distract me? Isn't this a waste of time? Why cloister myself in this cave of a train compartment? What if we lose time and are unable to make it up? For as the old railroad saying goes, "A late train only gets later." What if I become preoccupied with time and waste time worrying about time? Do I have enough books to keep me occupied? How do I pray when I'm forced to do nothing else but pray?

Will the words I read, like the words I heard the retreat master preach, seem foreign to me, not what I feel or experience? Will some person or book tell some interesting or funny stories? For stories always made retreats memorable for me when I was a teenager. I could enter the stories as I often could not enter the exhortations, however cogent they seemed.

In the club car five teenagers are talking nonstop, at least two of them are, the others listening, offering grunts from time to time. What would happen if they all stopped talking, turned inward? What would they find? What would I find? The emptiness is what we fear. We people our emptiness with fantasies, sexual or otherwise.

But why turn inward in the first place? It is evident these teens thrive on one another, on their relationships, their giggles, their story telling. A young African American woman is recounting, almost line by line, the film, *The Color Purple.* "I loooove that movie. I know it backwards and forwards." I believe her. The others are enthralled. She's a natural actor. Whatever would she need to turn inward for? Should she? Wouldn't that make her ill? And why didn't it make me ill to make a retreat as a fourteen-year-old boy in a Catholic seminary fifteen hundred miles from my New Mexico home?

The teenagers are playing cards, laughing, talking. How long has it been since I played cards, laughed, wasted time?

Was I precocious or weird or both to have actually enjoyed that first retreat? I remember looking forward to the retreat master's conferences in chapel, and I loved reading Father Isidore O'Brien's *Life of St. Francis.* I suppose reading made the retreat for me. A *Life of St. Francis* and in chapel, *The Imitation of Christ.* And behind everything was the dream that God would speak to me, that God would call my name, as God called Samuel in the Bible.

From that first deep prayer-experience till now, I cling to the hope of God calling my name, telling me my prayers have been heard, God revealing the secret of life, what it means, who I am in God's sight, how I will live forever. My first retreat as a young teenager was on some level the search for immortality, though it was probably not as important then as it is now that I am in my sixties.

⟨⟩

Spiritual Discipline and the Liturgical Year

My passage from the lay life to religious life in the Franciscan Order embraced not only the one-year novitiate after we graduated from high school and at the end of which we made temporary vows of poverty, chastity and obedience, but it included the three subsequent years—our first three years of college—in preparation for our final vows.

We spent those years at Duns Scotus College in Southfield, Michigan, a suburb of Detroit. The friary/college was named for Blessed John Duns Scotus, a medieval Franciscan philosopher/theologian, and the college life we lived from 1956 to 1960 was indeed medieval. Our lives were regulated by a strict monastic schedule originating in the Middle Ages that involved rising at 5:30 A.M. and repairing to chapel by 5:45 for the Angelus, a prayer honoring the Annunciation to the Virgin Mary by the angel Gabriel, and for morning meditation, which began always with the father guardian knocking on the wood of his choir stall, signaling all of us to kneel and recite the prayer of our holy father Saint Francis, "We adore you, Most Holy Lord, Jesus Christ, here and in all your churches which are in the whole world and we bless you because by your holy cross you have redeemed the world," followed by Saint Thomas Aquinas's prayer, *"O Sacrum Convivium in quo Christus sumitur, recollitur memoria passionis ejus, mens impletur gratia, et futurae gloriae nobis pignus datur"* ("O sacred repast in which Christ is consumed, the memory of his passion recalled, the mind is filled with grace and a pledge of future glory is granted to us"). The very fact that the latter prayer was in Latin, as were the hours of the Divine Office and the Mass itself, indicates a time before the Second Vatican Council, which opened the doors for liturgy to be sung and recited in the vernacular.

Following these brief prayers and a period of meditation, all would rise, again to the knocking of wood, and the master of clerics or the father guardian would intone, *"Deus in adjutorium meum intende,"* to which we would all respond, *"Domine, ad adjuvandum me festina"* ("God, come to my assistance," "Lord, make haste to help me"), and we were thereby launched into Prime and Terce, two morning prayers of the Divine Office, the whole of which were chanted to a single note (*recto tono*) that changed pitch from psalm to psalm according to the organist's modulations.

At 6:30 A.M. Conventual Mass would begin at the main altar, usually a so-called High Mass *sung* and with six candles lit to distinguish it from Low Mass that was simply *recited* with two candles lit. Simultaneously side-altar Masses were being celebrated at the various altars that lined each side of the church on the laity's side of the sanctuary, the main altar being in the center of the church separating the choir, where the friars attended Mass and recited the hours, from the laity's side of the church. Thus, there was a definite divide between the laity and religious, as we were officially termed by the canon law of the Catholic Church.

High Mass was sung in Gregorian chant from the *Liber Usualis*, a collection of chants for every day of the liturgical year, beginning in Advent (the four weeks before Christmas) and progressing through Christmas, Epiphany, so called Ordinary Time, the forty days of Lent, Easter, Pentecost (fifty days after Easter) and again Ordinary Time. All of these seasons were marked by dramatic changes in the color of vestments the priest wore and of the altar coverings, the presence or absence of flowers on the altar, the use (or not) of incense, even to the covering in purple of all statues and images in church during Lent and their uncovering on Holy Saturday Eve (the night before Easter Sunday), thus dramatically signaling the joy of Christ's Resurrection on Easter Sunday.

Color, smell, the passage of inner seasons corresponding to the seasons we experienced in nature, the constant sound and rhythm of plainchant, the repetition of rituals handed down for centuries—all of these sensory and spiritual rites formed who we were becoming as young religious who were simultaneously pursuing a bachelor's degree in philosophy. Again here the emphasis was on medieval philosophy centered on the Franciscan school, personified especially by Blessed John Duns Scotus and Saint Bonaventure.

At 7:10 A.M. we recited Sext and Nones, two further hours of the Divine Office, and at 7:45 we processed to the refectory—a beautiful medieval room with heavy tables lining each side exactly as in Medieval and Renaissance paintings of monastic refectories. At 8:00 there was private study and at 8:30 classes began—classes mainly in the liberal arts: mathematics, chemistry, biology, philosophy, history, economics, sociology, psychology, religion, English and American literature, composition, speech and Gregorian chant. Philosophy courses ran the gamut from logic to epistemology, cosmology, metaphysics, philosophical psychology and natural theology, resulting in almost sixty credits in philosophy with a minor in any of the liberal arts of our choosing.

Twenty minutes before lunch we would return to chapel for particular examen, or examination, and personal spiritual reading. The particular examen was a brief daily examination of conscience. Spiritual reading—ten minutes or so—consisted of reading prayerfully any spiritual book of your choosing. During this brief period over a year's time, for example, I read the entire Bible in the then newly published Ronald Knox translation from the Latin Vulgate edition of Saint Jerome.

Lunch was at noon, during which there was a period of silence, the only voice that of a reader (we all took turns) perched in an aerie of a pulpit high above the room proclaiming first a passage from Scripture, then the Latin ordo (the order of Divine Office for the day) and then reading from a spiritual book that encompassed a spectrum of texts, from a life of a saint to a travel book like H. V. Morton's *A Traveler in Rome*. After ten or fifteen minutes, the father guardian would ring a bell and pronounce, "*Deo gratias*" ("Thanks be to God"), to which we would respond, "*Deo gratias*," and conversation would begin.

After lunch we would again process two-by-two to chapel for "*statio*," a medieval ritual whereby we would all kneel before the Blessed Sacrament and pray aloud six Pater Nosters, Ave Marias and Glorias, with our arms outstretched in a cruciform position.

Classes resumed at 2:00 P.M. and continued till 3:30, when we broke for study, library work, walks in the woods, naps, showers and so on, until 5:00 P.M., when we returned again to chapel for Matins and Lauds, lasting until 5:40, followed by a brief meditation period until 6:15, when we processed two-by-two to the refectory for supper, during which there was again public reading and "*Deo gratias*," the permission to talk, or not, depending on times and seasons. The seasons of Advent and Lent, for example, were times when we were less likely to enjoy conversation at meals than at Christmas and Easter time.

After supper we processed two by two for "*statio*" again, after which we usually watched the evening news and walked around the grounds until 7:30 or so, when we retired to study until 9:30 and *magnum silentium*, the "great silence" that was kept until after the Conventual Mass the following morning. At 10:30 all lights were to be extinguished for the night.

I'm sure to most this rather rigid schedule must seem almost antediluvian, especially for eighteen- to twenty-two-year-old men. Even to me, at this remove from those days, it does seem extraordinary that we actually lived that way for the years of our spiritual formation, which lasted not only for the four years of undergraduate work at Duns Scotus College but also for the four years of graduate work at St. Leonard College, in Dayton, Ohio, prior to our ordination to the priesthood. And yet at the time it did not seem strange or unusual, but rather what one did to prepare for the priesthood and for life in the Franciscan Brotherhood. The schedule was both formative and moderating of impulses that could have led either to bizarre behavior or to sloth in one's pursuit of holiness or to laxity in spiritual discipline.

We were in the Franciscan Brotherhood because we believed we had a vocation, a call to be there. The schedule of our daily spiritual, intellectual and physical discipline was intended to nourish and discern that vocation. Some left and some persevered in the Franciscan vocation, but all attained a deep appreciation of and need for a liturgical life, a life centered on the church year—that calendar of feasts and seasons that celebrates and reenacts and puts us in touch with the mysteries of salvation. We learned to live simultaneously in two worlds, symbolized by the two calendars we followed, the one beginning January first and the other beginning on the first Sunday of Advent, which led us through the life of Christ and of the church.

In one sense, then, our whole nine years of preparation for the priesthood—from the novitiate to ordination—was a sustained period of liminality in which we were neither in the world nor out of the world but on the edge of both conditions. We were being purified and prepared to carry with us into the world we would enter as ministers everything we had learned of the interior life. When we enter our daily prayer today, we bring to our silence and solitude all the interior discipline learned during those years.

The liturgical year is a powerful ongoing recreation and remembering of the *Magnalia Dei*, the "Great Works of God," in history and in our individual lives. Using the liturgical year as a paradigm, I see our day-to-day lives in Ordinary Time, Advent and Lent as prolonged spiritual retreats, followed by the great seasons of praise and thanksgiving, Christmas, Easter and Pentecost.

The liturgical year provides a structure for the movement of the heart to God. It motivates and inspires and is a vehicle of grace. It reminds all people of the need for structure of some kind to nourish, moderate and maintain the impulse toward the spiritual. That which endures submits to the life-giving, structured practice of prayer and love. Haphazard, intermittent responses to spiritual impulses or grace soon wither and die, and the heart goes elsewhere.

Holy Orders: An Inner Album

Good Friday, 1948. I am standing on the front step. The muslin chasuble blows in the New Mexico wind. In front of me kneel seven children, boys and girls, Anglos and Mexican-Americans. I am inviting them to rise and come forward for the adoration of the cross. I am eleven years old.

Between that histrionic performance—and all the "Masses" I said as a child dressed in vestments my mother made at a play altar with its own little tabernacle draped in lace curtains—and the Mass I offer this morning at Pleasant Street Friary in Cincinnati, lies the story of my priesthood. I look at another old photograph of me playing Mass at a makeshift altar in the rented house on Fifth Street in Gallup. It looks strikingly like the makeshift shrine in my room here. We are who we were.

I can't remember when I didn't want to be a priest. There was a time, of course, that I had other images of what I would be when I grew up. There are, for example, photos of me "cooking" as a three-year-old in Silverton, Colorado. I'm standing in the backyard snow with pans all around me. That was before the snapshots of me in cowboy boots and Levi's, a white Stetson hat scrunched down on my four-year-old head. I'm at the Bodo ranch in Durango, Colorado. I don't remember those times, though I remember the World War II soldier times when I was six or seven, but by then the image of myself as a priest was the most vivid snapshot I carried around in my imagination.

That was before the Second Vatican Council, so the picture is of me in fiddleback Roman vestments, with a marble Romanesque altar. In this imaginary photo, I am standing with my back to the congregation, reading Mass in Latin. Other priests are offering Masses at side altars that line the walls of the church. At the rear on each side of the church are confessionals we enter every Saturday, the purple stole of penance around the priest's neck. The whole ambit of priesthood somehow arcs back and forth between altar and confessional. At first, I didn't have mental pictures of me elsewhere, though I knew priests did more than offer Mass and hear confessions.

Why, I wonder, is offering Mass so vivid a picture? Did it have something to do with the theater of it all? In a small New Mexico border town in the early 1940s, the priest at the altar must have seemed so special, so removed from the mundane, blue-collar lives of coal miners and railroad workers. The gold-brocaded vestments alone would have fired an imaginative young boy's dreams. Then there was the respect the priest was given in our Mexican, Spanish, Italian, Croatian world. He was somehow elevated, different, worthy of emulation.

Or was it something magical, mystical? I recall the dizzy feeling of kneeling in the small church of St. Francis of Assisi in Gallup thinking it is huge because I am little, overcome with the scent of lilies, the swirling incense, the profusion of lights and candles washing the altar cloths whiter, the priest in his gold vestments for Christmas or Easter, his chasuble sewn of spun gold, his shoes polished bright, his hair as white as the alb he wears starched stiff and proper by the white-wimpled sisters.

The ecstasy of it all—like a young athlete caught up in the rhythm, the movement of a Michael Jordan setup and shot, or my father listening on the radio to an announcer doing a blow-by-blow of a Joe Louis boxing match. That identification with the ideal, that sense that you *are* the other. You are Joe DiMaggio or Barry Bonds batting your last homer of the season. You are the priest ascending for the first time the altar of God, caught up in the dynamic of what you admire and love.

And so it probably began, the first inkling of a vocation, later to be clarified and solidified when I began in Junior High to drive the car for the Hospital Sisters of St. Francis who had come west from Springfield, Illinois, to minister to the poor, the sick and shut-ins. Through these sisters the image of Saint Francis working with the lepers took shape in my mind, and I knew that I, like the priests and sisters in my hometown, could only be a *Franciscan* priest who would one day live among the poor. That, too, has come to pass, though life in inner-city Cincinnati looks different from the 1950s images I had of living a Franciscan life with the poor.

Though in some ways generic, the memories of a priest's seminary days and those of his priesthood are unique to him, to the way God prepared him for ministry and the way he has chosen to live out that ministry in the church. The time of my own leaving for the seminary is a photograph of war ending in Korea, of Dwight Eisenhower as president, of the McCarthy era just beginning and of me reading Thomas Merton's *Seven Storey Mountain*. Though I was only fourteen years old, Merton's book held me enthralled. All the places he had seen and where he was born and the Kentucky monastery where he was living seemed like faraway, fairytale places to a boy growing up in New Mexico, longing to travel, to experience what he'd read about.

And so I left Gallup and never batted an eye or thought twice about the distance geographically and emotionally between Gallup and Cincinnati because that is what you did in those days if you wanted to be a priest—you went to the high school seminary wherever it was. And everyone congratulated you and was proud of you, except maybe your parents, who tried desperately to understand but still thought it was too soon to leave home and were probably right as parents seem to be in the long run. But I would hear none of that. I was in love with the idea of becoming a priest and wanted to give my life to God.

Thus began the journey from the mountains and desert of my youth to enter a seminary steeped in turn-of-the-century German immigrant traditions. Though my roots were in the American Southwest and, beyond that, in Northern Italy on both my mother's and father's sides of the family, I eagerly embraced the rather Prussian regimen of the seminary because it was so perfectly suited to what I was about: becoming a saint by erasing my past, putting on the garments of penance and embarking, with the earnestness of youth, on the long and arduous journey to the mountain of God. Asceticism itself became the god I'd hoped to meet on the mountaintop.

I set out, as spiritual manuals urged, by mortifying my palate: no desserts, no overeating at table, no eating between meals. It is not my rather priggish moderation, or even the mortification of the palate that amazes me so much today as the excesses to which I went in trying to be moderate. Somehow from all the pious literature I was reading at the time, I became convinced that if I yielded to even the smallest pleasure of the palate, I would fall into other sins as well.

Such ascetical exaggeration could have made my adolescence a miserable, tortured time. But strangely, it was not. It was filled with the sweetness of spiritual consolation and deep love for Mary, the Mother of God. I spent hours before her altar each week, and I lived in a world of incense and stained glass and countless *Lives of the Saints* that I read avidly, the way teenagers usually read comic books. Spiritual books were the real depository of God for me. They held God, and if I could only enter them, I would enter into God.

This conviction began with reading Thomas Merton prior to entering the seminary. Merton was there at the beginning of my conscious life in God. He, like me, had been looking for God. Like him I longed to know God, to find God. I didn't know where to look, though I had church and prayer and the Franciscan priests at our little parish in Gallup. I didn't look in the obvious places where most people would look, though I went to Mass often and even dropped into church to pray before the Blessed Sacrament.

I didn't expect to find in churches what I was looking for, because what moved me, was real for me, was the printed word. Books. Books drew me the way the Blessed Sacrament of the Body and Blood of Christ drew a saint into the Divine Presence. For me, almost literally, "In the beginning was the Word" (John 1:1). And that Word I had found in a book, *The Seven Storey Mountain*. I wonder how much of it I understood back then? Rereading it now, I'm sure I must have missed most of the references Merton makes to contemporary events, people, literary works, including the title's allusion to Dante's *Purgatorio*. What I did understand and what kept me reading was that Merton's words were of God. The one who wrote them had found the God I was looking for, the God who preoccupied me. And that God was somehow in the book Merton wrote, if only I could hang onto the feelings *The Seven Storey Mountain* provoked in me.

But God is not confined to books and the feelings they evoke in us. This a priest must know, and this God taught me in the only way I could learn. It all started when I entered the novitiate and began the retreat prior to donning the habit of Saint Francis. I had prayed for this moment, prepared for it, all through the high school seminary years, when most other teenage boys were learning about relating to girls, about living in "the world." From the moment I entered the novitiate in August 1955, following graduation from the high school seminary, all consolation ceased, all religious sentiments, all joy; and I was left without the felt presence of the God I thought I carried in my back pocket like the books that made God present to me. In desperation I reached for my faithful books, but God was no longer there.

It was then that God began the slow process of rebirthing me that I had tried so desperately to avoid, to bypass with pious words. I began to experience that dark night of the soul I'd read about and could so glibly assent to intellectually as a way to closer union with God. But now my resistance to this "self-sweat of spirit," as the poet Gerard Manley Hopkins names it, all but drove me mad. I was convinced I was spiritually arid and psychologically depressed because I had done something sinful, that I hadn't done enough penance, that God was angry with me, and so I increased my penances, unwilling to admit that maybe this was God's work, that God was leading me to a deeper relationship with him in the only way that I would hear. There was nowhere to go, no trains leaving for some ideal world, no place to escape from myself. I had to begin anew.

Since nothing I read was any help or gave any comfort or peace, I stopped reading for a while, and the light of my spirit went out. It would take eight slow years to counter the fleet four years of my running from God into a false piety and spirituality that kept the Word from becoming incarnate within me.

Eventually, I began to read not *books*, but *authors* I trusted; and the more philosophically and theologically "sound" they were, the more I trusted them, though never did I give myself over into their power as I had those other writers of my boyhood like Saint Thérèse of Lisieux, Saint Louis de Montfort, Thomas à Kempis and the early Thomas Merton. I analyzed authors now and argued with them and tested everything against my own experience of the "absence" of God in my life. God revealed himself in sacraments and the Word. Period. It had nothing to do with feelings. God was not a "spiritual experience." You just believed. You didn't try to stir up enthusiasm by reading pious literature; you read books like von Hildebrand's Liturgy and Personality, Dom Chautard's Soul of the Apostolate, Romano Guardini's The Lord.

Faith was all. Faith was gift. But what had taken place within was a subtle substitution of an intellectual world for the world of the emotions, the world of mind for the world of sentiment. The mind proved to be only a further escape, more subtle, more dangerous than the previous illusion that strong feelings indicate the presence of God's grace.

A dogmatic, doctrinaire attitude more often than not reveals a repressed personality rather than a person certain of his or her convictions, a self in hiding, rather than a self firm in a given faith. I thought, for example, that I was so pure and chaste, and in one sense I was, but for the wrong reasons and certainly not in a healthy way. I was becoming asexual, a pure little mind walking around looking like a man. Like others before me, I was deceived by my own self-anointing. My own mind's "orthodoxy" had led me away from a lived orthodoxy, which is always incarnational, always about men and women, not angels. I did not know it then, but I needed to become a human being before I could become a real disciple of Jesus Christ, the *Incarnate* Son of God.

What I praised about the sacraments, their merging of matter and spirit, I denied myself. Bread and wine became the Body and Blood of Christ and remained bread and wine in appearance and taste and function, but body somehow had to become spirit before it was holy.

This is an extreme stating of what I lived and believed at that time, and had anyone asked me, I would never have given intellectual assent to such a Manichaean stance. But practically, on the day-to-day level of living, that attitude was informing my action and non-action in a way I would have been ashamed to admit.

Of course, in a remembrance of things past, we are selective in what we remember and how we remember. The years of my preparation for the priesthood were not wholly preoccupied with the fear that I would never again find the God who fled my books and was now somewhere in hiding. Other things were happening as well, and the work of God within me and around me was having as great an impact on my day-to-day life as were my own fears and whatever else was motivating me in a conscious, compulsive way. I was living my life from day to day, following the schedule, doing what my spiritual directors assured me was the only way to proceed in spiritual aridity, namely, pray and work as if you felt the presence of God and God's presence would return. They assured me that in continuing to be faithful to my daily routine, just as I would were it bringing me deep consolation and peace, I would indeed find again deep consolation and peace. This *modus vivendi*, they all agreed, is the test of true love of God: to love God for God's own sake and not for what God can do for you. To persevere in spiritual discipline despite the lack of any feeling or consolation is the supreme detachment for one seeking the face of God. And so I continued to fulfill the offices of a once passionate love that I no longer felt. I submitted to the daily routine of the rather monastic *horarium* of the four years of college that began immediately after the completion of the year of novitiate. We made our temporary vows of poverty, chastity and obedience and then went on to Duns Scotus College for the four years of our undergraduate liberal education.

Through all my college years, faith alone carried me through, faith, especially, that I wasn't just putting in time and would never move beyond this arid plateau on which my spirit was marooned. My anxiety arose from the fear that I was going nowhere spiritually. I wanted the vows to lead somewhere, prayer to go somewhere, but I saw pride raising its head again and I, fortunately, listened this time to my spiritual directors rather than passages in books. I surrendered to what seemed an empty routine, I kept what seemed empty vows, and, paradoxically, that surrender led to God's return, just as my mentors had said it would.

In surrendering to the daily routine of our Franciscan life together, I was embracing the wisdom of centuries of spiritual formation. And since the ministerial priesthood is a way of life as well as a sacrament, I realized I must embrace my whole self, and not just a "spiritual" self. And in so doing, I was given back redeemed everything I had feared was lost forever. And it was Francis of Assisi who led me back, just as he had led me away as a boy. Back then I rode the bus out of town as on a white and gleaming steed to conquer in myself and others the Evil Enemy, as Francis of Assisi had ridden into battle against Perugia, the neighbor and enemy of Assisi. He rode forth to master and destroy the evil that was coming at him from "out there" somewhere, from outside himself.

Then one day Saint Francis met a leper on the road, and he realized that life wasn't about mastering at all, but about being mastered, surrendering to God when we meet God on the road. And God may not have the face we imagined, as Saint Francis learned when one day while he was still living "in the world" he dismounted his horse and approached a leper standing shame-faced in his path. He went up to the leper and embraced him and Francis' heart was filled with joy. He was no longer afraid. And as he mounted his horse to leave, he turned to wave to the leper, but there was no one there. He realized he'd embraced the Lord himself in embracing the rejected, the marginal person.

Furthermore, in embracing the leper, Francis was also embracing what he was afraid of in himself, what he had not yet reconciled in his own heart. He wrote in his Last Testament, "When I was in sin, the sight of lepers nauseated me beyond measure; but then God himself led me into their company, and I practiced mercy with them. When I had once become acquainted with them, what had previously nauseated me became a source of spiritual and physical consolation for me."

Through Saint Francis, then, as I grew to know him better, I realized that what God was showing me throughout my boyhood and early youth was that I was my own leper, that I needed to embrace myself and no longer fear the truth that I am a man, not an angel. And that is what I did in heart and mind and soul. And my own fears began to turn into spiritual and physical consolation for me.

Nor was this transformation just an intellectual exercise; it was made in the body, my own body and Christ's. It meant being able to look at myself in the mirror—not just from the neck up as in a "head trip," but to look at my whole self in a full-length mirror—and to see there that I was made good and beautiful in God's sight. And not only to see, but to celebrate what I saw.

The reality of the Incarnation had become real for me. What I'd known intellectually for years, I now felt in my bones, my blood, my heart. God is a flesh-and-blood human being, Jesus Christ. Jesus who had a body like mine, Jesus whose body is now glorified as mine will be if, like him, I embrace my whole self and love through it, with it. This transforming truth is, I believe, a *sine qua non* for the ministerial priest if his life is to be a "sacrament," a sign of the sacrament of holy orders he embodies.

Even my prayer changed. Jesus was now a living, breathing human being whose feet I kissed, with whom I conversed, laughed and cried. His wounds became emblems of my own previous fear and suspicion of the body that God made holy in his own flesh. The body was not separate from the soul, the body was enfleshed soul.

I stumble in trying to render that insight, that "epiphany" and the implications it had and has for how I now live and minister as a priest. I now *am* my body. It is the tangible expression of my soul, my immortal being, just as the tangible, human Jesus *is* the God whose essence and eternal being I cannot see. As Christ Jesus is the sacrament of the living God, so my body is the sacrament of who I really am, an ensouled person created by God to live forever.

My transformative experience was as though Christ had somehow been awakened within me, as in this moving poem by Symeon the New Theologian, a Greek Orthodox abbot, theologian and poet, who died in 1022.

> We awaken in Christ's body
> as Christ awakens our bodies,
> and my poor hand is Christ. He enters
> my foot, and is infinitely me.
>
> I move my hand, and wonderfully
> my hand becomes Christ, becomes all of Him
> (for God is indivisibly
> whole, seamless in His Godhood).
> I move my foot, and at once
> He appears like a flash of lightning.
> Do my words seem blasphemous?—Then
> open your heart to Him
>
> and let yourself receive the one
> who is opening to you so deeply.
> For if we genuinely love Him,
> we wake up inside Christ's body
> where all our body, all over,
> every most hidden part of it,

is realized in joy as Him
and He makes us, utterly, real,

and everything that is hurt, everything
that seemed to us dark, harsh, shameful,
maimed, ugly, irreparably
damaged, is in Him transformed

and recognized as whole, as lovely,
and radiant in His light
we awaken as the Beloved
in every last part of our body.[1]

The transformation so beautifully expressed by Symeon is not something that happened suddenly and dramatically in me. In fact, I have no memory of a moment, a "revelation" that something had changed in me. It was simply something that happened over time in the process of praying and living and trying to fulfill the obligations of being a Franciscan friar and later, after a further four years of graduate school and ordination, of being a Catholic priest. The same is true of anyone who continues to pray and tries to fulfill the obligations of love, whatever way of life (single or married, nun or religious brother or priest) that one has embraced.

That is why I am sharing this protracted personal memoir: its dynamic is, I believe, the dynamic of God's working in every soul. The so-called spiritual life is *God's* work within us; our work is to respond to that divine activity by trying to discern what God is doing within us, listening to the word God speaks in that action and learning to love others by first learning to love ourselves as whole persons.

This may mean learning first of all to forgive ourselves. The story of my own inner journey to the priesthood is precisely that journey of self-forgiveness to self-love to love of others. It is the story of everyone who enters upon the inner journey to that center where God is "heard" in silence and solitude as transforming love calling us to love ourselves and others as God loves us.

It was only after this prolonged inner journey that I was ready—if anyone is ever ready—to be ordained a priest.

❧

It is 1964. I can still feel his thumb, thick and firm in my palms. The smooth oil, slick with grace. My surprise at the soft flesh of this man ordaining me a priest. Surprise because he has spent two and a half years as a Japanese prisoner, a year and a half of house arrest after the Communist takeover in 1949 and twenty-eight months in a Chinese Communist jail. He was brought before a firing squad in a mock-execution staged for cameras and propaganda, its ruse unknown to him, standing there in the blast of camera shutters, and he still alive and well, wishing he was with Jesus in paradise. And perhaps he was, from that moment on. How can I, kneeling here in the lull of all this soft sacramentality, even dream to emulate a living martyr-bishop whose pudgy Polish thumb is signing me a priest forever?

I heard him speak twelve years before when I was a fifteen-year-old seminarian wide open for martyrdom and heroic sanctity—our idealized adolescent contribution to the Cold War. His voice, as he sat beneath the proscenium arch of the seminary study hall stage, came, it seemed to me, from deep within solitary confinement, a single light bulb, a steady drip of water and a bucket reeking of feces and urine—the sacraments of his personal crucifixion. He talked of how he worked out mental logarithms to keep sane, that and reciting all the poems he'd memorized as a young seminarian. I chose the poems, fearing logarithms would only insure madness in me. He kept simple rules for health and happiness: Talk less . . . listen more; look at TV less . . . think more; ride less . . . walk more; sit less . . . kneel more; rest less . . . work more; self less . . . others more; hate less . . . love more; eat less . . . live longer.

But his words of asceticism are eclipsed by the tangible memories of ordination: the anointing with holy chrism, a sign of the special anointing of the Holy Spirit who makes fruitful the priest's ministry; the presentation of the paten and chalice, the offering of the holy people which he is called to present to God; and the essential rite of the sacrament of holy orders: the bishop's imposition of hands on the head of the ordinand and the bishop's specific consecratory prayer asking God for the outpouring of the Holy Spirit and the Holy Spirit's gifts proper to the priestly ministry. And all of this grace mediated through hands that had been tied behind this bishop's back, through eyes that had been blindfolded, as he prepared to die for the same Christ whose priestly ministry I am entering.

We are at the liminal moment of the closing of Vatican II; the bishop's consecratory prayer is still in Latin. It loses something in translation, but even in English it moves me today, some thirty-five years later:

> Lord, fill with the gift of the Holy Spirit
> him whom you have deigned to raise to the rank of the
>   priesthood,
> that he may be worthy to stand without reproach before
>   your altar,
> to proclaim the Gospel of your kingdom,
> to fulfill the ministry of your word of truth,
> to offer spiritual gifts and sacrifices,
> to renew your people by the bath of rebirth;
> so that he may go out to meet
> our great God and Savior Jesus Christ, your only Son,
>   on the day of his second coming,
> and may receive from your vast goodness
> the recompense for a faithful administration of his
> order.[2]

It is the almost physical memory of anointing and hands on my head and words heard in the heart that I live within now fifty years after I played priest on our front steps that windy Good Friday when I was eleven. Even the sacrament of penance enacted in the dark of the confessional box, screen between priest and penitent when I was first ordained, is now made face-to-face, often ending with a signing of the cross on the penitent's forehead or a resting of my palms on the head of one bowing in profound contrition. The same palms in which I still feel the anointing oil and warm touch of Franciscan Bishop Rembert Kowalski.

Sacraments are like that: physical signs and signings that impart grace, which is most inward and profoundly spiritual. The physical is all we perceive; the spiritual is evident only in the metamorphoses that take place in our lives: the faith, the hope, the charity we cannot explain by means of purely human reason. That is the world in which I live as a priest: the physical as sign and promise of the spiritual. There is no polarity because the physical is all we see and hear, taste and touch and smell, for that *is* spiritual. The spiritual in the physical. God in bread and wine; God in water and oil; God in the consummation of married love; God in the anointing of the forehead of the baptized with sacred chrism in confirmation; God in comforting oil on the cool or burning forehead of the sick; God in the hearing of sins and in the words of absolution.

The forms of these actions, the language, too, may change; the physical dimension will not. For the Catholic Christian God is Incarnate and all redemption involves the physical: birthing and maturing, the dying and rising of the body, one day to be united forever with that inspiriting reality we call the soul.

The Mass is the very center of a priest's life, the Ur-text of all the texts he lives by. He does not write the Mass; the Mass writes him. In the end the priest becomes the text he utters at Mass. His is the body broken, the blood poured out for God's people. The same is true for *all* who offer the Mass with the priest. It is their body broken, as well, their blood poured out. The heart of the mystery of the Mass is that each person's offering is subsumed in the eucharistic bread and wine become Christ, the perfect offering to God.

Because the ministerial priest is chosen by a unique ordination and consecration to preside at the table of the Lord, the priest bears a commensurate responsibility to become Christ the priest, the one whose whole life is patterned after the Christ of the Last Supper, who consoles and prophesies, who breaks the bread and shares the wine with those at supper, who washes the feet of the apostles.

The words of Saint Francis to his brothers who are priests ring in my ear:

> If the blessed Virgin is so honored . . . since she carried Him in her most holy womb; if the blessed Baptist trembled and did not dare to touch the holy head of God; if the tomb in which He lay for some time is so venerated, how holy, just, and worthy must be the person who touches Him with his hands, receives Him in his heart and mouth, and offers Him to others to be received.[3]

And then, as is typical of Saint Francis, a paean flows from his mouth:

> Let all humankind tremble
> all the world shake
> and the heavens exult
> when Christ, the Son of the living God
> is present on the altar
> in the hands of a priest.
> O admirable heights and sublime lowliness!
> O sublime humility!
> O humble sublimity!
> That the Lord of the universe,
> God and the Son of God
> so humbles Himself
> that for our salvation
> He hides Himself under the little form of bread!
> Look, brothers, at the humility of God
> and pour out your hearts before Him!
> Humble yourselves, as well,
> that you may be exalted by Him.
> Therefore,
> hold back nothing of yourselves for yourselves
> so that
> He Who gives Himself totally to you
> may receive you totally.[4]

The ecstatic nature of Saint Francis' words may not quicken modern hearts, so de-sensitized have we become to anything less than the sensational. These are ecstatic words that pulse from the heart of mystery which some tend to demythologize and explain away as the last gasps of an age of faith.

And yet, and yet . . . it is the task and burden of the priest as we move into the third millennium to reaffirm mystery and ecstasy, to prophesy the coming of the Cosmic Christ in simple realities like bread and wine and ordinary human beings become God-like through the same bread and wine become God.

The priest is himself one of the faithful. Moreover, he is ministered to even as he ministers, for all of the baptized are a holy priesthood among whom the ministerial priest is ordained to symbolize and do in a unique way what all the baptized do: make present the kingdom of heaven. The kingdom of heaven is within, and the unique sacramental, evangelizing and prophetic role of the ministerial priest is to make the kingdom within visible.

When I played Mass as a child, I was putting on a mini-drama that imitated what I saw the priest doing. Now when I offer Mass, I am not just acting; I am presiding at God's reenacting of the whole mystery of salvation—the passion, death and resurrection of Christ—in the transubstantiating act of bread and wine becoming the Body and Blood of Christ through the action of the Holy Spirit, who is always the primary actor in the sacraments.

☙

Fifty years after I stood playing priest on the front step of our home, I stand at the altar of St. Francis Church, Gallup, New Mexico, where I sang my first Mass. They are still here, the Croatian, Italian, Spanish, Mexican, Native American faces that prayed with me when I was a boy. We are all graying, a bit slower, and I no longer assume a place above them as I stand before the altar. My back is not turned toward them as I face the altar; we gather together around the altar as we offer this Mass in a shared priesthood we were all made more aware of by the Second Vatican Council. My ministerial priesthood is still radically different in kind from our shared priesthood, but their and my perception of how I exercise that priesthood has changed.

I am still liturgical leader of this gathering we call church, but the emphasis is now on the sacrament of the church itself, and not on the priest. Our relating is reciprocal to an extent that was unthinkable in 1948. These faces that were then on the other side of the communion rail and sanctuary now stand in the sanctuary and proclaim the readings of the daily liturgy. They pronounce, "The Body of Christ," as they distribute Holy Communion; they take the Holy Eucharist to the sick of the parish. Some are ordained deacons who proclaim the Gospel at Mass and preach, who preside over funerals, who assist in the distribution of Holy Communion and in the blessing of marriages.

I find words for what I feel standing here today in Pope John Paul II's, 1990 Holy Thursday letter to priests: "The priesthood is not an institution that exists alongside the laity, or 'above' it.

The priesthood of bishops and priests, as well as of deacons, is 'for' the laity, and precisely for this reason it possesses a ministerial character, that is to say, one of 'service'."[5]

To better understand how I stand at the altar differently today from when I "said" Mass as a young ten-year-old boy, a brief historical overview of the Catholic understanding of priesthood may be helpful. Patrick J. Dunn, in his book, *Priesthood: A Re-examination of the Roman Catholic Theology of the Presbyterate*, has provided an excellent summary outline. Dunn maintains that very early in the church the distinction between clergy and laity appeared. By feudal times clerical society paralleled civil society, with its own courts, its own laws, it own officials. By the time of Pope Leo I (d. 461), laity were referred to as *ecclesia discens*, "the listening church." Already in the sixth century, the priest "said Mass" on behalf of the people; Mass was viewed as a sacrifice in which the Body and Blood of Christ was made present, offered for the sins of the people and consumed in Holy Communion.

The Mass as it looked in the tenth century was the Mass I grew up with all through childhood, adolescence and early manhood until my ordination and the advent of Vatican II. That is the Mass as a liturgy of sacrifice and supplication, rather than communion, thanksgiving; it is performed by a single priest and not by a bishop surrounded by his college of presbyters; it is done *for* rather than *with* people; it is spoken in Latin and not the vernacular. Also, by the Middle Ages the priesthood itself is increasingly bound to Eucharist—priests are ordained primarily for the celebration of the Eucharist. From the Council of Trent in the sixteenth century until today, the Catholic belief is that ordination confers a sacramental spiritual power that permanently distinguishes the priest, and what he does in the sacraments he does by that power and not by any delegation from the community.

The Council of Trent links the priesthood even more to cult: *Sacrificium et sacerdotium ita Dei ordinatione coniuncta sunt,* "Sacrifice and priesthood are conjoined by ordination of God." The great achievement of Vatican II in the 1960s was to liberate the priesthood from the limitations of this definition and to free ministerial service in the church from being the exclusive prerogative of the clergy. It reintroduces the New Testament term, *presbyter*, for "priest." The term *presbyter* means "elder" and has more collegial and fraternal associations than does the term *sacerdos*, which means "priest." The vision of Vatican II is this: the apostolic preaching of the gospel convokes the people of God who offer themselves to God as a "living sacrifice." Through the ministry of presbyters the spiritual sacrifice of the faithful is made perfect in union with the sacrifice of Christ, as the Eucharist is offered in the name of the whole church. For Vatican II the presbyterate reaches its climax in the celebration of the Eucharist, which is by contrast the starting point for the Council of Trent.

But for all this broader view and different starting point, Vatican II still teaches that eucharistic sacrifice is the center and root of the whole priestly life, and the real presence of Christ in the Eucharist is unequivocally reaffirmed.[6]

⟨❧❧⟩

Pictures, images, rise in my mind: Moses, his arms supported by Aaron and Hur because "Whenever Moses held up his hand, Israel prevailed; and whenever he lowered his hand, Amalek prevailed" (Exodus 17:11). This was a battle. It went well when Moses' hands were lifted in prayer. This image comforts me at the altar and in all my priestly ministry. I am a priest called from among the body of the faithful who are themselves priests. I am the one chosen to offer sacrifice and prayers with them. I am the visible symbol not only of their priesthood but of *the* Priest, Jesus Christ. But I am weak and sinful; I grow weary if not supported by the priesthood of all the faithful. I do not raise my hands alone—Aaron and Hur, Rebecca and Sarah, are holding up my arms. There is that reciprocity in the fullness of ministerial priesthood: I am the one chosen, anointed, from among the baptized, to be the visible sign of their own priesthood and (in what makes ministerial priesthood unique) the visible sign and representative of Christ, Priest of the New Covenant. The ministerial priest acts sacramentally in the person of Christ by reason of holy orders, the sacrament which incorporates one of the baptized into the order of those who, with the bishop, continue Christ's mission of priest, prophet, servant.

Another image, more disturbing, arrests my attention. I find it in the *Selected Poems* of the Polish poet, Zbigniew Herbert. The poem is dedicated *to the worshipers of deceased religions*.

The Priest

A priest whose deity
descended to earth

In a half-ruined temple
revealed its human face

I impotent priest
who lifting up my hands
know that from this neither rain nor locust
neither harvest nor thunderstorm

   —I am repeating a dried-out verse
   with the same incantation
   of rapture

A neck growing to martyrdom
is struck by the flat of a jeering hand

My holy dance before the altar
is seen only by a shadow
with the gestures of a street urchin

   —And nonetheless
   I raise up eyes and hands
   I raise up song

And I know that the sacrificial smoke
drifting into a cold sky
braids a pigtail for a deity
without a head.[7]

No image distills for me so clearly the way I and other priests feel from time to time: that sense of despair and cruel comedy, that feeling that you are a pathetic marionette or clown making absurd gestures at an altar whose God is, alas, no longer there, or at least, no longer listening. You stand seemingly naked and vulnerable trying on the words that now seem utterly true and not just pious echoes of the words of the Savior on the cross: "My God, my God, why have you forsaken me?"

This image begins to dissolve into another that resolves Herbert's macabre image—macabre, but hauntingly true when faith yields to despair. I am walking the streets of Assisi one summer evening. I come around a corner and literally run into a little man who smiles and says, to my amazement, "I'm your brother, Francis." I wonder momentarily if I have run into Saint Francis himself. In a way I have. His name is Francis but he is English—from Nottingham—and he is a diocesan priest, neither of which would fit the non-English, non-priest, Saint Francis. And yet, as I am to learn, his is the spirit of Saint Francis pressed down and overflowing.

Years before he came to Assisi to die, but while praying in the Basilica of St. Francis, he was given to understand that he was to throw away his pills and gather the scraps that fell from the Lord's table. And so like the stories of hagiography, he threw his pills away and waited for a further word.

One day (as legends often begin) he was walking the piazza in front of the basilica when he saw a young man dejected and forlorn, and he knew, as he had known before while praying in the basilica, that here was the scrap he was somehow to gather. He went up to the boy and said, "I am your brother, Francis. Come with me and I will show you how to pray." And so began Father Francis Halprin's real ministry, he who thought his ministry was over.

Several years and thousands of young men later, Father Francis found me, like all the others, in Assisi. He told me of his first conversion from a successful pastor to a man broken and suffering from an emotional collapse, shunned by everyone but his dog and a prostitute who brought him a meal from time to time. From emotional collapse to a subsequent physical collapse from cancer, he found his way back to Assisi, where as a struggling artist he had come as a young college student to study the frescoes of Giotto. A priesthood and a life away he returned to die and ended up caring for the scraps that fell from Christ's table, his "little brothers," as he called them, young men he would take in—five days at a time—and teach them to pray. His daily Mass at the Basilica of St. Francis, his prayer, his "little brothers."

Such was his life until he died a few years ago in his eighties. Such is the life of any priest: his Mass, his prayer, his brothers and sisters to serve as the Lord himself shows him.

"No one showed me what I should do, but the Most High Himself revealed to me that I should live according to the form of the Holy Gospel," Saint Francis writes in his Last Testament. That form of the gospel, for the Franciscan priest or the Franciscan in spirit like Father Francis Halprin, is expressed by Saint Francis in the same Testament: "While I was in sin, it seemed very bitter to me to see lepers. And the Lord himself led me among them, and I worked mercy with them. And when I left them, that which seemed bitter to me was changed into sweetness of soul and body."[8]

The ministry of the Franciscan priest, whatever its external configuration—from pastor to teacher to chaplain to writer to administrator to preacher to whatever avocation his ministry embraces—is a ministry of working mercy with those who are or who perceive themselves as on the margins, rejected, despised by others. The Franciscan priest ministers *with* rather than *to* these scraps from the Lord's table: "I worked mercy with them," Saint Francis says so tellingly.

The church where I most often work mercy today is a small arched chapel built of trust and listening and discerning. It is the church Jesus speaks of when he says, "For where two or three are gathered in my name, I am there among them" (Matthew 18:20). There are usually only two who enter this chapel, I and another person who has entered this sacred place to discern God's will.

This chapel is named variously, but most often it is called Spiritual Direction, a name that can be misleading if either I as priest or the person seeking direction thinks that I have something called "spiritual direction" as a kind of gift of ordination that I then impart to the other. Spiritual Direction is rather a sacred space that we two enter together in order to discern God's will for the one seeking God's direction.

Everyone who comes to me for spiritual direction already has a direction, a configuration of his or her life, because of who their parents and ancestors are, where they come from geographically, what decisions they've made or failed to make, what they've suffered, and most importantly for this sacred relationship, why they've entered the Chapel of Spiritual Direction. Together we will discern the pattern of God's working in their lives up to this point, what it is they are seeking now, and what they are to do in order to respond to this new movement—where, in other words, God is leading them in the immediate future.

The Chapel of Spiritual Direction is located quite near the dwellings of psychotherapy and counseling, and often, one seeking spiritual direction is simultaneously visiting those other dwellings, as well—all in order to know where one has been, where one is and where one's future lies.

What makes the Chapel of Spiritual Direction doubly rewarding and important to me is that within this sacred space I am further empowered to sacramentalize the sharing enacted here. If confession of sin is a dimension of the sharing, I am ordained to forgive that sin in the name of the One who dwells there with us. Because of this sacramentalizing of the person's sharing, there is the liberating knowledge not only that one has finally shared something profoundly personal in a sacred and safe place but that one is forgiven.

I've added here the words "safe place" in describing this chapel because they involve the bulk of the work that I do here as priestly minister. I do not give direction; I discern with the person the direction God has already given and is now giving. I do not preach; I listen. I do not exercise authority; I bow in reverence before the mystery of God's authority over the one before me—the authority of unconditional love. What I *do* is try to build the chapel itself: a safe sacramental place where God dwells and God's unconditional love is the listening ear.

⚜

It is Christmas morning. I stand at the altar in the chapel of the cloistered Poor Clare nuns. The altar is oak, beautifully crafted by one of our Franciscan brothers. The chapel and monastery are in the woods of the former high school seminary I attended as a teenager and where I later taught for twelve years. It is a new monastery founded a few years ago. There are five Poor Clares gathered for Christmas Mass. A small group, a microcosm of the whole church.

Through the large ceiling-to-floor windows that fill the entire convex wall of the sanctuary, all of nature seems ready to enter here. Deer cross nearby, and squirrels punctuate the silent oak trees.

All of creation is an immense sacrament. All created things are signs of God that we decipher in order to find our way to God. The medieval Franciscan theologian, Saint Bonaventure, puts it this way: Every creature is a word of God. *Verbum Divinum est omnis creatura.* This is so because they are created by God and because *the* Word, the Second Person of the Blessed Trinity, becomes one with all of creation in the Incarnate Christ.

But in order to see God in all things we must see with a purified vision. The work, or practice, or *ascesis* of purifying one's vision is characterized by medieval theologians as the threefold way of purgation, illumination and union. In the Franciscan tradition that has formed me, this threefold way consists of recognizing and overcoming sin, imitating Christ and surrendering to union with God as the Beloved Spouse of the soul. These ways are recursive, in the sense that each way is found within the others and intertwined with them. The soul is never fixed on a single way.

Nor is it possible or helpful to try and determine what particular way one is in. All three exist simultaneously, and the only marker I have found helpful is that one way seems to predominate at a given time in one's life. What that way is can usually be discerned like this: In the purgative way there seems to be a somewhat equal distribution of personal effort and God's grace; in the illuminative way more emphasis is given to the imitation of Christ; and in the unitive way the major component is grace, pure gift.

Another way of saying this is that souls are on three ways at the same time, ways that are beginning, progressing and perfecting stages. As I see it, all three ways are operative in the reception and living of the sacraments. Baptism and reconciliation have much to do with the recognition and overcoming of sin; confirmation, matrimony and holy orders enable us to imitate Christ in his ministry, or as Saint Francis puts it, in following in the footprints of Christ. Imitating Christ for Saint Bonaventure means living out one's life with Christ as the exemplar or template of how to live in the world as in a sacrament of the Divine.

The anointing of the sick and especially the Holy Eucharist are the sacraments of contemplation as surrender to union with the Beloved. In the Eucharist all of creation becomes sacrament in the signs of bread and wine. In surrender to the healing touch of Christ in the anointing of the sick and in surrender to the action of the Holy Eucharist contemplative union with the Beloved is attained.

The configuration of our inner life is the configuration of the lived sacramental life of the church. And as that configuration reveals more and more the image of Christ in us and among us, the more our vision sees Christ in all of creation. We begin with the sacraments, we live them, we begin to see sacramental signs everywhere, we end up becoming ourselves "sacraments" of God's presence.

SOURCES FOR THIS CHAPTER

Being a Priest Today, Donald J. Goergen, O.P., ed. (Collegeville, Minn.: The Liturgical Press, 1992).

Catechism of the Catholic Church (Washington, D.C.: United States Catholic Conference, Inc., Libreria Editrice Vaticana, 1994).

A Concert of Charisms: Ordained Ministry in Religious Life, Paul K. Hennessey, C.F.C., ed. (New York/Mahwah, N.J.: Paulist Press, 1997).

Francis and Clare: The Complete Works, Regis Armstrong, O.F.M. CAP., and Ignatius Brady, O.F.M., eds. (New York: Paulist Press, 1982).

Priest: Identity and Ministry, Robert J. Wister, ed. (Wilmington, Del.: Michael Glazier, Inc., 1990).

The Spirituality of the Diocesan Priest, Donald B. Cozzens, ed. (Collegeville, Minn.: The Liturgical Press, 1997).

NOTES

[1] From *The Enlightened Heart: An Anthology of Sacred Poetry,* Stephen Mitchell, ed. (New York: Harper and Row, 1989), pp. 38–39.

[2] *Catechism of the Catholic Church* (Washington, D.C.: United States Catholic Conference, Inc.; Libreria Editrice Vaticana, 1994), #1587.

[3] *Francis and Clare: The Complete Works,* ed. by Regis J. Armstrong, O.F.M. CAP., and Ignatius C. Brady, O.F.M. (New York: Paulist Press, 1982), p. 57.

[4] Author's translation.

[5] John Paul II, *Holy Thursday Letter to My Brother Priests* (Princeton, N.J.: Scepter Publications, 1994).

[6] See Patrick J. Dunn, *Priesthood: A Re-examination of the Roman Catholic Theology of the Presbyterate* (New York: Alba House, 1997).

[7] Zbigniew Herbert, *Herbert: Selected Poems,* Czeslaw Milosz and Peter Dale Scott, trans. (New York: The Ecco Press, 1986), p. 23.

[8] *Francis and Clare: The Complete Works,* p. 154.

PART TWO:
The Middle Way

The Church Year

It is Advent—the time of waiting, of expectation. It is the start of the church year, which begins with the birth of Christ and proceeds through all the events of his life, his passion, his death, his resurrection and ascension into heaven. Fifty days following the Resurrection of Christ the church celebrates Whitsun or Pentecost (from the Greek word for "fifty"), the feast of the descent of the Holy Spirit into the disciples of Christ. From Pentecost to Advent is termed Ordinary Time, the time of our daily, ordinary living-out of the mysteries of Christ, which we celebrated from Advent to Pentecost. With Advent the waiting for Christ's new birth begins again.

Thus, year in, year out, the Christian reenacts and relives the life of Christ, who is the church's model of how to live one's life. As the apostle Paul puts it,

> He is the image of the invisible God, the firstborn of all creation; for in him all things in heaven and on earth were created, things visible and invisible, whether thrones or dominions or rulers or powers—all things have been created through him and for him. He himself is before all things, and in him all things hold together. He is the head of the body, the church; he is the beginning, the firstborn from the dead, so that he might come to have first place in everything. For in him all the fullness of God was pleased to dwell, and through him God was pleased to reconcile to himself all things, whether on earth or in heaven, by making peace through the blood of his cross. (Colossians 1:15–21)

All of Christian asceticism and spirituality is the endeavor to pattern one's life on the Christ defined and illumined in the above extraordinary paragraph. It would be difficult to overemphasize the centrality of Christ in the life of the Christian.

Whatever the belief, whatever the prayer-practice, the morality, the daily living, if it is not a reflection of Christ, then that belief, that action, is not God-like, and therefore not holy. It is as simple and as difficult as that. For as Jesus himself says to his apostles at the Last Supper, "When the Spirit of truth comes, he will guide you into all the truth. . . . He will glorify me, because he will take what is mine and declare it to you" (John 16:13–14).

It is not surprising that the whole of the Christian's life is modeled on the church's liturgical year, which is itself modeled on the mystery of the incarnation, life, passion, death, resurrection and ascension of Christ. Nor is it surprising that the various Christian denominations are separated precisely in how they see and interpret Christ, the head of the church. For how one understands the head determines the look, the configuration, of the body, the church. Christians understand that they are collectively the Body of Christ. Who Christ is, therefore, and what he teaches is central to each Christian denomination.

Prayer for a Christian, then, is a more intense and protracted time of entering (through silence and solitude) into the mystery of Christ. Lent, for example, is a participation in the time of prayer which Christ himself made in preparation for his public ministry—the forty days he spent fasting and praying in the desert.

And all, as in Advent, is in the waiting. Waiting for the church year to unfold, waiting for the mystery of Christ to unveil some of its hidden countenance, waiting for one's own transformation into Christ, waiting for the Second Coming of Christ. But all this waiting is more than waiting, for as the Christian waits, he or she also lives out the life of Christ and thereby is gradually being transformed into the image of the Christ he or she is waiting for.

The Christian does not wait passively for the life that is to come, as if the present life does not matter. On the contrary, the present life is the stuff of divinity, the world already transformed by the Incarnation. Because Christ is the enfleshment (incarnation) of the living God, and because he lived among us as one of us, everything human has been redeemed and sanctified by Christ. And just as Christ descended from heaven into this world and then ascended again to heaven having taught us how to live in this world in order to follow him into heaven, so each person, so to speak, descends from heaven when God breathes the soul into each one of us at our conception. The soul, God's life within us, then directs how we are to live our life in order to return to the God who created us. When we die, our soul returns to its Maker to await the resurrection of its body when Christ comes to reclaim the earth at the end of time. Even after the end of one's life on earth there is waiting.

And so we return to the beginning, to Advent, the time of waiting, that sets the pattern of our prayer. We wait in humility and patience, entering every day into the mystery of Christ's life that particular day invites us to meditate on. We enter into the liturgical readings of the day and wait in silence, with no expectations other than the hope that God will speak to us through the readings, through the silence.

Something Else

What of the person who is outside any structured religion, and yet is drawn to enter into prayer, who wants to become a more interior, spiritual person? I believe the same dynamic works here as that of the liturgical year with its ongoing rhythm of retreat and celebration. However, instead of meditating on and remembering within a structured religion the Magnalia Dei, the great works of God throughout the history of a given people, the non-churched person meditates on and celebrates the manifestations of God's workings in his or her own life, his or her own family, or period of history.

As for the religious person, there may be times of increased awareness or spirituality, as in the following experience of the poet, Alfred Corn.

> I had just emerged safe from a situation that I rightly felt to be a close brush with death. It was a sunny midday in early spring. I was taking a walk in the Grove Street Cemetery in New Haven, a self-described atheist out enjoying the first pink-and-white blossoms on the cherry trees. I sat down on one of the flat tombstones, squinting in the sunlight as I placed a tape cassette of Bach keyboard music into a portable player. A four-voiced fugue began playing, brilliant strands of harpsichord counterpoint interweaving a golden sonic tapestry superimposed over the grass and trees and sunlight I was seeing. And suddenly I knew with complete certainty that the world and everything in it was a Creation, so complex as by contrast to simplify the Bach fugue into a child's bare, unaccompanied nursery song; but that Bach, too, had had a similar intuition and did the best he could, by heaping harmonic complexity on melodic intricacy and formal rightness to convey, however incompletely, some no-

tion of the universal order and its greatness. I felt the sun and earth revolve around each other, the irresistible tug of grass, tree, and creature toward light and heat, the interweaving of earth breezes, sky, and something else in perfected counterpoint, and myself at the heart of things simply allowing these sensations and intimations to play through me. The ground beneath, holding the bones of those who died in earlier centuries, the invisible action of earthworms, roots, and moles, was like a flowing river, as flexible as the breezes, as permeable as the sky, the bass notes of the immense opus that God—yes, I was forced to see—had made. The sun sent brilliant iridescent shards of light through my eyelashes as I squinted and squinted, trying both to normalize and to accept the moment as it happened. This was an "in the body" experience, but it was also a period of *ekstasis*, or ecstasy, which I cannot—I speak as a fool—convey completely. Nor was it the last of its kind.[1]

Say that one has had a similar experience. The inclination of the heart is surely to remember and savor that experience. One's prayer, then, will have something to do with taking time to recreate the circumstances wherein that unsolicited experience happened. Maybe it will happen again, maybe not. In either case, you are remembering in a more structured way, you are meditating on the effects of the experience, you are celebrating and giving thanks for something that was pure gift, which is the definition of grace.

Or perhaps, as with most of us, there has been no spiritual experience such as that recorded by Alfred Corn, but you are still drawn to quiet, solitude, even prayer, if only you knew how to pray. Here, too, the dynamic is the same. You quiet down, find some solitude, in order to consider more intensely or more at length what this impulse within is, and where it comes from. You may even enter into a structured, communal prayer group or worshiping community in order to explore what it is about and to learn whether or not your own spiritual inclinations are similar to those of others, both those who've had spiritual experiences and those who have not but who, like you, are searching. Then should something happen, tangible or intangible, to bring you peace of soul, or simply to further pique your curiosity, you will want to return again to remember, celebrate, meditate further, give thanks or just to know again the peace of silence and solitude itself, apart from any so-called spiritual experience.

You may enter into prayer simply because it helps you slow down, experience a measure of personal space not invaded by the demands of others, listen to your own heart again. And that, too, is prayer. That, too, involves remembering or experiencing for the first time a dynamic that seems fairly universal for those who enter into prayer in or outside established religion.

NOTES

[1] *Incarnation: Contemporary Writers on the New Testament,* Alfred Corn, ed. (New York: Viking Press, 1990), pp. 131–132.

Jesus

J esus. How problematic he is for many. How distorted his image by some Christians who have politicized and trivialized the mystery of the Incarnation until "Christian" has come to mean a right-wing, rigid, self-righteous prig, or a liberal, ever politically correct reed shaken by whatever wind is blowing. Christianity devoid of the mystery of Christ and the profound Judeo-Christian intellectual/mystical/liturgical tradition; Christianity, in short, devoid of its culture, cultura, cult, becomes instead a vehicle for my own prejudices, philosophy, fears, whatever.

Christianity is the mystery of Jesus Christ, not a political party or a personality type. Mystery is approached on one's knees, not on a soapbox; in the tangle of one's own mind and heart, not in clear, simplistic answers or a Polyanna-like bleeding-heart sympathy. It implies reverence, silence, listening and, above all, prayer, both communal and private. Mystery is not conveyed in harangues; it is felt in the humble listening of the heart, sensed in the mind's prayerful approach to sacred texts, the soul's trembling before the transcendent made tangible in Jesus Christ, the Word made flesh.

Without mystery and attendant reverence, Christianity becomes as loud as everything else in a world gone mad with exposure, prurient curiosity and invasion of the sacredness of all things.

And having said all that, I sound as strident, opinionated and self-righteous as those whose attitudes I'm decrying. Which is precisely what happens when any of us begins to get his or her "licks" in. What I am doing here is how wars begin, and persecution, hatred, separation of peoples. We begin to judge, from a supposed position of superiority, moral or otherwise. True wisdom brings together, includes, is compassionate. Nowhere has the healing power of compassionate, wise love been more beautifully articulated than by Saint Paul, himself at times quite a haranguer, though not in this exquisite passage, so well known, so little lived:

If I speak in the tongues of mortals and of angels, but do not have love, I am a noisy gong or a clanging cymbal. And if I have prophetic powers, and understand all mysteries and all knowledge, and if I have all faith, so as to remove mountains, but do not have love, I am nothing. If I give away all my possessions, and if I hand over my body so that I may boast, but do not have love, I gain nothing.

Love is patient; love is kind; love is not envious or boastful or arrogant or rude. It does not insist on its own way; it is not irritable or resentful; it does not rejoice in wrongdoing, but rejoices in the truth. It bears all things, believes all things, hopes all things, endures all things.

Love never ends. But as for prophecies, they will come to an end; as for tongues, they will cease; as for knowledge, it will come to an end. . . . And now faith, hope, and love abide, these three; and the greatest of these is love. (1 Corinthians 13:1–9, 13)

What is of God changes hearts, brings peace and love. No matter how great the miracle, how intense the spiritual high, it is nothing more than hysteria, wish fulfillment or projection, if it does not make me a more compassionate, loving human being. The measure of all spirituality is charity, the charity defined by Saint Paul in the preceding passage.

The Middle Way

The one who prays can be deceived into thinking that we enter into prayer in order to get zapped somehow with spiritual power and thereby bypass the hard work of living a virtuous life. Holiness is hard work, but it also is gift. I must, as Saint Teresa says, work as if everything depended on me, pray as if everything depended on God. The Pelagian heresy asserts that I acquire my own salvation; I merit it somehow. Quietism claims that I don't have to do anything. Virtue, contemplation is given to me simply by waiting around in quietness of heart. The truth is somewhere between. As the old medieval adage has it, *"In medio stat virtus."* "In the middle is virtue."

The middle way is what prayer and contemplation help us to see. We make the effort to pray, we submit to its discipline, its silence and solitude. We try to quiet our hearts, try to believe there is something, someone transcendent who is also immanent and who loves us with a Creator's love. That part is our work. The rest is God's. And God's part is gift. We have made the effort to be in a space of receptivity. Whether anything of God happens there depends on God.

And no matter what seems to be a deep spiritual experience, it is not, if we are not more charitable because of it and ultimately more at peace. Ultimately, because for a time God's work in us can be very distressing, throwing us into confusion and turmoil. Something is being purified, something clarified; or some deep-rooted destructive habit or attitude is being transformed into virtue. This can be painful; this can take a long time. But in the end the transformation brings peace of soul and a charity that reaches out to others, especially the poor, the rejected, the despised.

Spiritual goodness is manifest not in spiritual highs, but in human acts that are unselfish, generous, compassionate. Acts that make others feel validated, affirmed, special. Mother Teresa of Calcutta often recounted how a man she lifted out of the gutter and held in her arms as he died, said, "I have lived like an animal; I'm dying like an angel." On the other hand, false spirituality, selfish do-gooding, makes the other feel less, judged, patronized, unworthy, especially if the object of our so-called charity is someone who has never experienced God's presence in a tangible, transforming way.

Another way of saying this is that no gift of God is solely for me. It's also for others through me. I am filled with the love or light of God so that those in darkness, those without love can know love through me. And the emphasis here is not on the "me" but on the "through." In selfless love, charity, I become transparent so that God's love can work *through* me. I get out of the way, so to speak, so that God can do God's work of affirming, loving, lifting up those with whom I come in contact.

Such loving begins to be patterned during prayer itself. There, as on a medieval pilgrimage, I am joined with many I do not know, have never met before, all of us together seeking to enter the same mystery of God's love for us, God's presence in everything made manifest when we take the time to slow down, look, listen, pray.

And we pray *together* even when we pray in solitude. For even in solitude we bring all of humanity with us on the solitary quest. I am I, but I also am humanity praying for itself. As John Donne has written so poignantly,

> No man is an island, entire of itself; every man is a piece of the continent, a part of the main. If a clod be washed away by the sea, Europe is the less, as well as if a promontory were, as well as if a manor of thy friend's or of thine own were: any man's death diminishes me, because I am involved with mankind, and therefore never send to know for whom the bell tolls; it tolls for thee.[1]

If everyone's dying diminishes me somehow, so does everyone's living affect my own, for we are all one in our humanity. As the contemporary Sicilian novelist Gesualdo Bufalino writes in one of his stories:

> The human condition, with all its prickles, its tundras of yellow boredom, at least has this to be said for it:

that it gives each of us a guarantee, signed by the mayor in person, of an indisputable identity; and while appointing us life-tenants of the cubic metre or so we occupy on earth, it does not thereby deprive us of the comfort of feeling at one with millions and millions of other far-flung human beings.[2]

NOTES

[1] John Donne, *Devotions Upon Emergent Occasions* (Ann Arbor, Mich.: The University of Michigan Press, 1959), p. 108.
[2] Gesualdo Bufalino, *The Keeper of Ruins,* Patrick Creagh, trans. (London: Harvill, 1994).

The Pasture Spring

*B*egin with breathing. Breathe in. Breathe out. You are aware of your breathing—not as a technique or a gimmick, but to focus on the reality that you are not only a breathing being, but you are being breathed. Breathing is not simply something you do automatically without thinking about it, but you are simultaneously being breathed by God, who breathes life into you: "...the Lord God formed man from the dust of the ground and breathed into his nostrils the breath of life, and the man became a living being" (Genesis 2:7).

Prayer begins here with the nostrils. You sit and focus on that place in your nostrils where the incoming air hits. It is here that God breathed life into you; it is here at this specific spot where God continues to breathe you. Awareness of yourself has led immediately to awareness of the Other. In prayer you follow this breath within to its source deep in your own center. There you discover that what you thought was coming from without is really coming from within, drawing everything into that sacred cell, that temple, that geography of inner mountains to climb. But what is drawn in is not held; it is expelled again, creating a rhythm of breathing in and breathing out.

Gradually you surrender awareness of breathing to the One who breathes you from within; you hold the image of God (whatever that image is for you) inside, letting that image dissolve into the reality of the One who is actually breathing you, letting what is imageless heal and renew you. Then you come out into the world around you.

This is a primary dynamic of prayer: entering in, abiding there a while, returning to the workaday world having learned a way of praying that gives energy and peace to daily life, provided we continue this practice every day. Then prayer, like an old habit we've grown accustomed to, sustains us when other habits alter or cease because of death or losses and separations that make us feel bereft and adrift. Lighting one's candle, calling upon God or saints or the spirits of loved ones gone before, anchors the soul. I am here once more in this place of prayer where I have known silence and the dark night of the soul, as well as the "ecstasy" of sensing the presence of the supernatural.

The place of prayer is not all sweetness and light, but the place where we have spoken with God in the fullness of human experience—in joy and sorrow, in darkness and light, in faith and doubt, in sin and grace, in ignorance and knowing—whatever we may have been experiencing at the time. We have returned and continue to return to this place because in prayer something mysterious always happens, whether or not we realize it at the time. Prayer is like a door that opens out into what we are afraid may not be there, the light, the voice that speaks to the heart, the silence that is more than silence. Prayer is the habit that sustains when the feelings and consolations, the inspirations and enthusiasms are no longer there. Prayer is opening the door every morning and every evening even when there is no one on the doorstep. Prayer is the hope that one day, if I continue to open the door, God, or God's messenger will be there to greet me. That opening of the door arranges my life, keeps faith and hope alive, and shows me the importance of a daily discipline if I am to make any sense of the muddle of life. Prayer is opening the door, sometimes no more than routinely, rather than the passage through the door into the eternal realms. Most of the time, if the door opens onto anything, it is to a vision or image of our own world transformed by the loving glance of God. We see how good our life is when we surrender it to God's light and love.

Learning to pray, then, becomes a crucial imperative for learning to live.

But how do I learn to pray? Can I learn to pray in my own home or in my garden or the park at the end of the street? I can, but it is more difficult for those who haven't a natural propensity or desire for prayer, or who do better when there are others gathered for the same purpose. The experience of primal peoples teaches us the important lesson that rites of initiation are important for any activity or level of consciousness that is to endure for the rest of one's life. For some, going to a monastery and joining in the prayer of the monks and nuns may be that sort of initiation; prayer is facilitated by the example and instruction of those already living the life of prayer. Or seeking out a spiritual director may also be helpful. Or simply being part of a praying community such as a local church or synagogue or mosque.

But with any practice, there are those who find their own way into prayer from the very beginning. This is true, for example, of Saint Ignatius of Loyola, the founder of the Jesuits, whose *Spiritual Practices* came out of his solitary retreat at Manresa in Spain.

To return to the comparison with the writing process, many contemporary writers have been initiated into the writing craft by writing workshops to which they return from time to time as to a source of inspiration and further refinement of their craft. Others, and these are often our great writers, never took a writing course or participated in a writing workshop, but they return again and again to their own source of inspiration, whether that be a place or a memory or an image or another writer whose work triggers their own creativity. These are the naturals, as we say, and the rest of us may need more than our own solitary muse to get us going, at least initially.

The same is true in the spiritual life. There are the naturals, but then there are the rest of us who need to be initiated into the practice of prayer. These pages, for example, endeavor to illustrate the dynamic of the prayer experience, not as a how-to manual that substitutes for praying, but as a companion for your own prayer, reassuring you that what you are experiencing is not weird or unusual, but is the experience of all practitioners of prayer.

The experiences related here are what I know of prayer and also what I continue to learn from others—what they find helpful. The dynamic is, I believe, common to all religious traditions, even though the object and content of the prayer-practice may differ.

To use a pastoral image from Robert Frost,

> I'm going out to clean the pasture spring;
> I'll only stop to rake the leaves away
> (And wait to watch the water clear, I may):
> I sha'n't be gone long—You come too.[1]

We're going into prayer together; you watch me rake the leaves away. What we see when the water clears depends on who we are individually. But that individual vision brings you and me back to the pool, back to clearing away the accumulated leaves.

NOTES

[1] Robert Frost, "The Pasture," frontispiece to *The Poetry of Robert Frost,* Edward Connery Lathem, ed. (New York: Henry Holt, 1979), p. 1.

Play

The modern temptation is to measure worth by work, by productivity. I am only as meaningful as the good work I do on this earth. The mystique of hard work and its payoff, success and self-fulfillment, infuses all of modern life, from the monk's life of prayer to the child's beginning the work of going to school at the earliest age possible. There seems to be little appreciation of leisure, of contemplation, even of rest. For when our work is done for the week, it never is. When the work we do for a living (the phrase itself is telling) is over, we begin the hard work of relaxing, working out, conditioning our bodies, building up our strength for more work. Everything, including relaxation, has to be a Herculean effort or it's somehow suspect.

Work as the ultimate value, is part of America's Puritan heritage, but such an attitude is also due to the gradual erosion of an appreciation of receptivity, of contemplation, whereby we relax long enough to see the world in a new way, the way of non-possession and non-domination, the way of the saint and the poet.

When we embark upon the practice of prayer, one of the first things we are aware of is that this is not some activity we are going to master so that we can come away with the best possible results. We can't say, "Okay, what do I do to get my money's worth here and have something tangible in my pocket?"

Prayer doesn't work like that. Prayer forces us to change our commercial attitudes that tell us if we work hard, we'll get what we're after. Prayer calls us to the leisure of simply being open and receptive to whatever gift God offers us in silence and solitude. And what we receive, what we come to know and experience in prayer is not something we can necessarily communicate to others who have not experienced the effects of a life of prayer.

We can easily say what we *did* in prayer, but it is not so easy to say what really happened there, what we really became aware of. Not because there is something esoteric or mysterious about the experience itself, but because the knowledge gained in prayer is often an intuitive knowledge, a knowing of the heart, of the soul, as well as of the mind. It is the kind of knowledge we get from poems and stories which is hard to paraphrase; all we can do is simply recite the whole poem again or retell the story, hoping this time the listener will get it without our having to try to explain it, which is like trying to explain a joke to somebody who doesn't get it.

Here, for example, is a story I once heard that says a lot about the knowledge imparted by prayer.

> There were two monks walking beside the Yangtze River in flood, looking for a safe place to ford the river. When they found a place that seemed fordable, there was a woman there, too, with her baskets, trying to cross to the other side.
>
> The first monk, seeing her, understood her fear and apprehension, and said to her, " Are you afraid to cross over to the other side?" She nodded. "Well, let us all three go across together. I will carry you on my back, and my brother here will carry your baskets."
>
> And that is how they all crossed the swollen river.
>
> Now when they reached the other side, the woman went her way and the monks theirs. But after the two monks had been walking in silence for some time, the second monk said,
>
> "Brother, why did you do that?"
>
> "Do what, brother?"
>
> "Cross the river with that woman. You know we're not supposed to have anything to do with women, and yet you not only spoke to that woman; you let her climb on your back and you carried her across the river."
>
> "Brother," the first monk said, "I left that woman at the river bank. Are you still carrying her?"

Now, the story either speaks to you or it doesn't. You either intuitively understand, or not. And the same is true of the subtler, wordless perceptions that happen in prayer. We are looking at a tree in the woods, or a flower, not analyzing it, but simply looking at it without any intention of possessing it through knowledge, and we suddenly take it in so that it becomes a part of our inner landscape.

The philosopher Josef Pieper describes this kind of knowing like this:

> What happens when we look at a rose? What do we do as we become aware of color and form? Our soul is passive and receptive. We, are, to be sure, awake and active, but our attention is not strained; we simply "look"—insofar, that is, as we "contemplate" it and are not already "observing" it (for "observing" implies that we are beginning to count, to measure and to weigh up). . . .[1]

This is the kind of intuitive knowing I experienced as a boy looking at the New Mexico night sky and which I wrote about years later in a college sophomore essay that began like this:

> I like to chance upon the stars, to take them by surprise and say, "I'm back again." I like to enjoy them with no scientific or philosophical intent, but just to stop and look. It all began with a boy and the stars of the New Mexico sky. I spent many hours with stars then. Yet every opportunity was a new experience, a new revelation. Still, I didn't spend all my time with the stars. Only a dark night could draw me away from the artificial lights of the city and make me look up and see the lights of the sky. The darker the night, the brighter they seemed, the more inviting their call.

This surrender to seeing and hearing without any illusions about hard work getting the results I expect is what happens in prayer. I begin to appreciate how much of what I receive is gift, gratuitous, given without my earning it. Or if there is hard work and effort, it is the hard work of not working so hard to get something to happen. But rather to relax, let go and just listen, look, let myself receive a gift—whatever comes from this experience of slowing down. I surrender work to leisure, doing and accomplishing to contemplation.

For some, "contemplation" can be a scary word. It conjures up mystics, visions, altered states. But in the sense I am using it here, contemplation is something we can all experience if we let ourselves be receptive to it. For to contemplate is, in Pieper's words, "to open one's eyes receptively to whatever offers itself to one's vision, and the things seen enter into us, so to speak, without calling for any effort or strain on our part to possess them."[2]

Perhaps what all of this adds up to is simply that we moderns have lost our sense of play. We no longer know how to play, unless play becomes a recreation that we have to work too hard at, squeezing it in between profitable work and watching TV.

Real play flows from celebration, and celebration is directly related to rituals of gratitude. Gratitude for a day of rest, gratitude for the fruits of the earth, for important events like birthdays and anniversaries, but especially, gratitude for divine events, ritual commemorations of God's revelations, epiphanies and saving acts.

More and more, rituals of gratitude and worship are as rushed and "squeezed in" as everything else that is not work related. Family rituals, too, suffer from the same anxiety that we are wasting valuable time we can't really afford. The pressures of work that seem never to end, that we take home with us, worry about, and that make us wonder when we'll be laid off, all create an atmosphere that is not conducive to celebration and play. What play we do engage in is directly related to being in better shape at work.

The decision to embark upon a prayer life, therefore, is an attempt to reverse this mad cycle of purposeful work. To step back and catch our breath, to slow down and try to get in touch with another more peaceful, more natural rhythm. The rhythm of the heart at peace. The rhythm of nature around us, of gestation. It is a decision to break free of the grip of modern industrial and commercial acceleration, to go aside and rest a while.

In prayer we listen to our own heart, to our own breathing. We let our inner movement lead us, rather than the demands of everyone around us. We treat ourselves to the play we only dimly remember from childhood. To pray is to begin again by stepping out of the mainstream for a while and "wasting time." It is a decision to try and recover our sense of childlike wonder and awe at how wonderfully we are made, how good is the God who made us and the world around us.

NOTES

[1] Josef Pieper, *Leisure, the Basis of Culture* (New York: Pantheon Books, 1952), p. 31.
[2] Ibid.

PART THREE:

The Secret Garden

The Secret Garden

Frances Hodgson Burnett's *The Secret Garden* is the story of Mary Lennox, whose parents die of cholera in India and who is sent to live with her uncle at his manor in England. Mary the Sour, Mary Quite Contrary, who is transformed by the discovery of her uncle's secret garden, which he has kept closed up and off limits for ten years because his wife died in a fall from one of the garden's trees. Mary's curiosity and her friendship with a robin (who finds the key while rooting for worms) lead her to the secret garden. She tends the garden with the help of Dickon, a peasant boy, a little "Saint Francis" who befriends and talks to animals. Mary and Dickon bring the garden back to life. And in the same way they restore, too, Colin, Mary's bedridden ten-year-old cousin who has been hidden away in the manor house, hypochondriachal, afraid he will be a hunchback and die rejected by his father who wants no sign of his wife anywhere. Mary finds Colin by snooping around the house and following his cries that echo from time to time.

Mary and Dickon bring Colin to the secret garden in a wheelchair and, by means of the Magic that makes the garden come to life, Colin, too, comes to life and Mary is changed from a nasty, disagreeable child to a happy child like Dickon. Colin's dramatic change begins the day the three children sit in a circle and Colin starts to chant a mantra over and over. "The sun is shining—that is the Magic! The flowers are growing—that is the Magic. Being alive is the Magic. The Magic is in me! Magic! Come and help!"[1]

Sometime later, the father, away from home and still grieving over his young wife's death, hears her voice telling him she is in the garden. He rushes home and finds the children there and is stunned to see Colin healthy and happy. Colin tells his father it was the garden that did it. "Take me to the garden, then, and tell me all about it," the father says. And the children lead him into the secret garden.

We all have our childhood gardens, our caves, our nests and attics and cellars. Hiding places where we daydreamed another life, where we were the heroes and heroines, where time stood still and we forgot to go home for supper, forgot that we were supposed to be somewhere else much less important than our dream world. And often it is these hiding places that rise to the surface when we enter into prayer.

In my own case I begin to meditate and remember, and I see a small boy, ten or eleven years old. He is sitting beneath a large sandstone rock across the dirt road from his home on North Fifth Street. It is night, the stars are out, and he is alone, staring at the sky . . .

That same boy sits high up in the recesses of Kit Carson's cave outside of Gallup. A slow drip of water plunks into a natural bowl hollowed out of the cave's stone. He is alone. It is scary there. But he remains, listening attentively, his eyes turned toward the mouth of the cave flooded with light that doesn't quite reach the spot where he crouches next to the pool of water . . .

The wind, the incessant wind. Sand blowing everywhere, spinning a cocoon around the young boy, insulating him from others, from a clear view of what's around him . . .

He's bundled in blankets, Vicks VapoRub stinging his nostrils, his mother's tender voice reading to him. It is safe under the covers. He is tired, feverish, but somehow comforted as well . . .

The Chief Theater on Coal Avenue. A double feature: Hopalong Cassidy and Charlie Chan. It is dark in the theater. There are other children and adults around him, but he doesn't notice. His eyes are fixed on the screen, his mind and heart are lost in the moving images cast by the projector's bulb. He's in another world . . .

These images also float across my mind's screen when I look at the word "retreat." I see withdrawal there, but I also see retreat, in the sense of treating myself again to images which conjure up funding experiences in my early life, times when my own well was being filled with water I would draw upon again and again.

I scan some of the *Oxford English Dictionary's* entries for "retreat" and each definition is a way into a personal memory: a moment, a place, an image brought back from my youth.

Retreat...—L. *retrahere* to draw back....The act of retiring or withdrawing into privacy, or into some place of safety....The act of withdrawing from society, public life, business or office; retirement, seclusion....A period of complete seclusion devoted to religious exercises. ...A place of seclusion or privacy....A place of refuge....A hiding place; a lair or den....The act of retiring or withdrawing in the face of opposition, difficulty, or danger.

Even as a teenager at the high school seminary, I had my secret gardens. Places in the woods where I would go to be alone, even a corner of a classroom on Saturday afternoons when winter was in the air and afternoon sports were over. I'd shower quickly and screw up my courage to go to the cloister door outside the second floor dormitory, look up Father Timon's number, two rings followed by three more, listen for his rapid footsteps, hold my breath and when he appeared at the door, I'd gulp and ask if I could borrow his record player. Despite his frown, he'd always say yes and I'd be surprised, as if he'd never said yes before.

He would let the door thud shut and emerge shortly afterwards holding a small portable player covered in a two-tone brown cheesecloth made to look like leather. He'd hand me the player in silence, then produce from under his arm held tight to his left side, the same two records: one, the Grieg *Piano Concerto* played by Artur Rubinstein and Rachmaninoff's *Second Piano Concerto* with Fritz Reiner and the Chicago Symphony Orchestra, and the other, Tchaikovsky's *1812 Overture* and *Capriccio Italien* with Eugene Ormandy and the Philadelphia Philharmonic.

How many winter Saturdays I spent on the snow-covered steppes of Russia brooding with Rachmaninoff or somewhere in Norway running brilliantly through fields and up the sides of hills with Grieg. Less often, I'd condescend to fight the war of 1812 or frolic in the grandeur of Tchaikovsky's Italy.

Though this was more an experience of imagination and the transformative power of music, it was not unlike what is experienced when we enter into a time of meditative prayer. Nor were my Saturdays with music unlike the earlier desert-and-sandstone days of my childhood when I would make shrines in the rocks that fronted our small stucco house. I was trying then to locate God and the saints just as later on I would try to locate peace of mind in classical music.

As a young boy, everything around me seemed windswept and plain. God couldn't be in so barren a place, I thought, and so I made shrines into which I would place a statue of Mary or a holy card of a saint. I would talk to them, and because they were statues or pictures, they were always calm and beautiful. Most of my childhood fantasies were of the lives of the saints—something of an embarrassment now. I remember reading Graham Greene's *The Power and the Glory* in college and wincing in recognition at the scene of the mother who is forever reading stories to her son from the lives of the saints in the desperate hope that her boy will be a saint, not a sinner like the whiskey priest or Padre Jose with his woman who dominates him.

With age and experience I grew out of those pious stories, but not out of what they represented. I may see God more in the rocks and sand today than in statues and holy cards, but I am still trying to locate God, to know with certainty what can only, for most of us, be known by faith, on the testimony of others. What amazes me is how I continue to long for God's face, as I did when I prayed to the saints or listened to music, hoping that between the notes an image of God might emerge.

Even now that I realize God's face is revealed in everything that is, I still long for some unique revelation, some granting of an audience, a glimpse of the One I have tried to love my whole life long.

I have experienced the transformation of parts of my life that I thought would never change. And that is all I really know. "The rest," as Horatio says in *Hamlet,* "is silence." Except for one thing more—the desire itself.

Perhaps the greatest evidence of God in one's life is simply that the desire for God has continued unabated. The desire is like the magic that restores Colin, the magic he believes in, that makes the flowers grow and keeps him alive. This desire has to be from some source beyond or it could not have been maintained in the face of doubt and years of spiritual dryness. In the end it is the desire that makes all the difference. The desire for God has kept me praying, kept me seeking, kept me sane. The desire is what I have that I know did not come from me. It has been there so long I wonder if I was born with it.

I have no memory of any special event that awakened this feeling within me, no luminous moment of revelation. I try to remember some divine epiphany. That, of course, is what we do, isn't it? We look for dates and times, for signs that something unique has just happened. And yet life rarely happens that way. We don't usually remember any specific incident that explains why we are the way we are, unless it was something traumatic that befell us. And even in such cases, we can suffer certain difficulties or problems for years, not knowing for sure when or where they began and—just as strangely—not knowing what made them disappear. Something of which we are unconscious works within us and has its own times and seasons, and all the interim is doubt and confusion and getting ahead of ourselves. The Spirit blows where it will; it comes and goes, apart from our bidding.

Ultimately, then, I enter into prayer out of unsatiated desire for the One who continues to be revealed partially and incompletely through everything that is. In prayer I work with those partial revelations, I let them hold me transfixed like the music of Grieg or Tchaikovsky or Rachmaninoff, I turn and become like a child again. I hope that, like Colin, I will be healed by the secret garden of my meditation, that I will be able to say, "It was the garden that did it—and Mary and Dickon and the creatures—and the Magic. I'm well! . . . I shall live forever and ever!"

NOTES

[1] All quotes in this section are from Frances Hodgson Burnett, *The Secret Garden,* retold by Jane Parker Resnick (Philadelphia: Courage Books, 1990).

Of Visions

Most of us don't know God except through symbol, parable, story. Mostly we know God through language, the testimony of others who have experienced God. As a boy beginning to wonder about God, I turned to my parents, to priests and nuns, and they told me about God. They directed me to the New Testament, to the catechism. I attended catechism classes, listened to God's word at Mass, read the lives of the saints who had experienced God.

All the while I was hoping God would speak to me as God had to others like Saint Paul, who was struck to the ground and in a flash of light heard a voice tell him, "get up and enter the city, and you will be told what you are to do" (Acts 9:6). And Paul, blind and confused, is led to Damascus where, after three days during which he neither eats nor drinks, he is led to Straight Street to a man named Ananias, who lays his hands on Paul and something like scales fall from his eyes and he can see and is baptized.

The experience of Paul on the road to Damascus and during those three days in Damascus, three days like the three days of Jesus' passion, death and resurrection, became a template in my mind, a picture of what it would be like if God were to come into my life with the same surety and power. It never happened quite that way, and yet God has spoken to me as surely as to Saint Paul. I know this, not in power or visions or blindness turning to sight.

In a more symbolic, yet real sense God has let scales fall from my eyes, too. The scales, mainly, of my expectations of what it would be like were God to speak to me. One day, years and years after I'd begun listening for God's voice and praying God would reveal himself, I realized that listening for God's voice had changed my life for the better. I had become wholly attuned to anything that would give me access to God. I listened and read Holy Scripture avidly, yet prayerfully. I talked to and listened to priests and all those entrusted with God's word: the pope, the church, the preacher at liturgy. I went to Mass as to *the* source of God's word, spoken and incarnated in the Eucharist, which gave me an intimacy with God as great as that of Saint Paul.

In short, the life I had been leading in search of and responding to God's word spoken in the church was proof that God had indeed spoken to me. The very desire for God came from God and made God present to me. And now when I attend or lead a weekend retreat, I realize this three-day experience is a replication of Saint Paul's three days in Damascus. God has led me and the other retreatants to come together in this place. God has done so in the very desire we all have for God to remove the scales from our eyes that we might see.

The effect of prayer is usually simply the desire to return and pray again because we sense that eventually something will happen. Then one day we realize what we were hoping would happen has been happening all along—we've become God-centered, God-desiring, and God-loving, and no extraordinary vision has been given us. God has been revealed in a desire that has changed the way we live our lives. It becomes clear to us that God is revealed in symbol, parable, story. Only now, that revelation is the story of our own life, itself a symbol and parable of God's working in an individual life.

There are moments, to be sure, of increased faith, for some even a powerful inrush of the Holy Spirit, resulting in gifts like the gift of tongues or healing or prophecy. But none of these gifts are as important as the ongoing desire for God, to know and love God with our whole mind and heart and soul. That desire alone transforms us into what we thought required some special revelation, some flash of light or audible voice.

Such visions, in fact, are problematic and can result from an over-active imagination at best, or psychosis at worst. They may or may not be of God, whereas the desire for God, maintained and nourished over a lifetime, is in the end the surest sign that God has spoken to us.

I believe the desire for God is what leads us into a life of prayer; the desire for God keeps us coming back to prayer; the desire for God gradually removes the scales from our eyes and we "see" in prayer that we already know and have been experiencing the God we've so desired.

Contemplation

The sacramental life of the Catholic Church is a ritualizing of the Divine Immanence. Bread and wine, water, oil, candles, incense, the consummation of married love, are all external, perceivable signs of grace, of the presence of God. We are pilgrims and strangers here only in that we do not yet see and understand that this is our true home, that heaven is all around us, as well as where we go to as we pass beyond the body into that which the body is a sign of.

The body is the external configuration of our unique soul. And the leaving behind of our body (to rise again, according to the Christian tradition) is the affirmation of our passing beyond the external reality that lay beneath all along. The poet Rainer Maria Rilke expresses beautifully the exile we feel because we don't know how to break through the images of God that conceal rather than reveal the God just beyond our deepest desire.

> You, neighbor God, if sometimes in the night
> I rouse you with loud knocking, I do so
> only because I seldom hear you breathe
> and know: you are alone.
>
> And should you need a drink, no one is there
> to reach it to you, groping in the dark.
> Always I hearken. Give but a small sign.
> I am quite near.
>
> Between us there is but a narrow wall,
> and by sheer chance; for it would take
> merely a call from your lips or from mine
> to break it down,
> and that without a sound.
>
> The wall is builded of your images.
> They stand before you hiding you like names,
> And when the light within me blazes high

that in my inmost soul I know you by,
the radiance is squandered on their frames.And then
my senses, which too soon grow lame,
exiled from you, must go their homeless ways.[1]

How interesting and revealing that Rilke says the images we have of God are a wall between us and God. They hide God like other walls we call "names." So that when the light within us blazes and is about to reveal God to us, these names and images come between and the light of our knowing is squandered "on their frames." And then our senses, lame when they are exiled from God, "must go their homeless ways."

What does this mean? Hasn't God revealed names to us, names that tell us who God is? And hasn't God given us images that help us "see" the Divine Person (images like "Divine Person")? And aren't these names and images revealed in words we call Sacred Scriptures, the divinely revealed writings of the great religions? And why would I quote Rilke, a modern German poet, and not these sacred writings?

I do so for two reasons. First, because we usually do quote these writings in talking about God, and secondly, because a subtle truth of the spiritual life is articulated by Rilke, a man outside organized religion, in a poem that approaches its truth the way only poetry can, with hints and metaphor and allusion. And that truth is that our images of God, our ideas and the names whereby we address God (another name), can sometimes dim and even extinguish the inner light that God enkindles within us through silent and imageless prayer. Instead of surrendering to this inner light, this revelation that rises from within, we feel compelled to name it, give it a face, relate it to the names and images of a given religion. And in so doing the mind and the ego kill that which is beyond mind and ego, that which it is best simply to receive in awe and thanksgiving and adoration, our senses thereby purified by what we surrender to, which cannot be named or imaged, except to say it is light and yet more than light. It illumines and purifies, and like a poem itself, cannot be translated or paraphrased; it can only be experienced.

Thomas Merton expresses it this way in a famous letter to Abdul Aziz.

Strictly speaking I have a very simple way of prayer. It is centered on attention to the presence of God and to His will and His love. That is to say that it is centered on faith by which alone we can know the presence of God. One might say this gives my meditation the character described by the prophet as "being before God if you saw Him." Yet it does not mean imagining anything or conceiving a precise image of God, for to my mind this would be a kind of idolatry. On the contrary, it is a matter of adoring Him as invisible and infinitely beyond our comprehension, and realizing Him as all. My prayer tends very much toward what you call "fana." There is in my heart this great thirst to recognize totally the nothingness of all that is not God. My prayer is then a kind of praise rising up out of the center of Nothing and Silence. If I am still present "myself" this I recognize as an obstacle about which I can do nothing unless He Himself removes the obstacle. If He wills He can then make the Nothingness into a total clarity. If He does not will, then the Nothingness seems itself to be an object and remains an obstacle. Such is my ordinary way of prayer, or meditation. It is not "thinking about" anything, but a direct seeking of the Face of the Invisible, which cannot be found unless we become lost in Him who is Invisible.[2]

In prayer we wait for the Other to break through our own preconceived images and naming words. And too often we are talking so much ourselves, or imaging the Other to whom we're talking, that we never stop and listen in silence. That silence, that listening, that patient prayer that is pure openness and receptivity is where we begin to hear what can't be heard, see what can't be seen. It is where we experience the Other who is all the names we know and all the images, too, revealed without a name, without an image. This is the prayer of contemplation.

Contemplation is an activity of body and mind, heart and soul that in the silence and solitude of the self waits patiently for a nameless, imageless visitation that reveals and transforms. Contemplation is something we can enter everywhere and any time we choose to enter the cell within. There, in silence and solitude, we wait in reverence and openness.

Sometimes we experience a breakthrough of the Divine, sometimes not. But always in prayer something happens which is part of the ongoing transformation of the self. This transformation is a gradual shining through of the soul, so that eventually the whole person becomes a living prayer, a further partial revelation of the God of names and images which are not God but which have become names and images in an attempt to name and image what we know transcends both.

NOTES

[1] Rainer Maria Rilke, *Poems from the Book of Hours* (New York: New Directions, 1941), p. 13.

[2] Thomas Merton, *The Hidden Ground of Love: The Letters of Thomas Merton on Religious Experience and Social Concerns*, William H. Shannon, ed. (New York: Farrar, Straus, Giroux, 1985), pp. 63–65.

Awareness

A formidable obstacle to prayer is the feeling that we are wasting time. We need to do something to fill up the time. The result is that we reach for books or spiritual exercises too soon. We don't sit in the silence or simply contemplate a scene or an object. We begin to seek God without listening, like someone who needs to talk incessantly instead of listening to the other and respecting the silences of any true dialogue.

We have learned this need for constant chatter from a society that fills up every silence with speech or canned music. From television we have learned that every pause, every soundless microsecond is costing somebody money. There must be sound. We then internalize the virtual reality of television and feel that our own lives need to be filled with sound and productive chatter. And so, in prayer we are unnerved by the silence; and often we compensate by substituting spiritual activity for our usual activity in order to avoid the sensation of wasting time, of not accomplishing anything spiritual in this precious time we have set aside. As a result, our prayer seldom brings us to the depth of receptivity necessary to retreat from the frenetic activity of our daily lives and arrive at the place wherein God speaks to the soul.

In Dante's *Divine Comedy* the poet does indeed enter the woods of silence, dark and wild, and there surrender to a three-days' journey—from Good Friday to Easter Sunday—into the depths of his own soul. What he sees and hears there, what he finds, resembles the content of the journey into prayer. First of all, he is accompanied by a guide, his mentor, the Roman poet Virgil, for the first two levels of his journey: hell and purgatory. For the deepest level, heaven, he is accompanied by his spiritual guide, the beloved Beatrice.

Who is your guide, your mentor? Whom do you trust to lead you into the depths of your soul? For me, it is usually Francis of Assisi, my spiritual father, for the deepest level of the journey. The first levels have been facilitated by different mentors, usually someone whom I find particularly helpful at a given time of my life. These mentors have ranged from Thomas Merton and Saint Thérèse of Lisieux to Dante and the Jesuit poet Gerard Manley Hopkins, from Thomas à Kempis to the poet Denise Levertov. I am drawn to poets because they, above all, lead me out of mundane seeing into a vision of the world that is fresh and deep, a vision that I know is only granted in silence. The poet's words come out of silence.

Second, Dante allows himself to be led. He relinquishes the need to control every step of the way. He risks the depths. We all realize that this entering into the depths of the self without proper guidance is a dangerous thing. We also realize that though we surrender to a guide's direction, we need to be free to say, "This is far enough. I can go no farther now." We need to know our own limits. Not everyone descends—or needs to descend—to the same depths. In other words, we don't have to descend to madness or to something terrifying. We need only descend to silence, to that center where listening is more important than speaking, patient waiting more important than performing any spiritual exercise.

This waiting in silent expectation for God's voice is *the* spiritual discipline—especially because God's voice is the silence itself. In total silence of heart and mind something happens that is a non-happening, something I know is God's voice because gradually my life begins to be transformed. I become more peaceful, more charitable, more profound in my response to life itself. I move from being a superficial person to being an interior person.

What I have written here may seem to denigrate spiritual exercises or vocal and mental prayer. It is not intended to do so. The point I am making is that prayers and spiritual exercises are not ends in themselves; they are means to that silence and listening that is a resting in the presence of God. Awareness of being in God's presence is the goal of prayer. From that awareness all else will flow.

The Hidden Treasure

The elements of the spiritual life are usually presented as knowledge, love, purification, union. And most writers put them in the same order. The problem for the novice in the life of prayer is that any sequence such as the above is often interpreted chronologically—first I know, then love, then am purified and, finally, attain union with the Beloved. But as in human love, the common elements of love's experience do not occur in neat, sequential, self-contained units. In each of these elements are facets of the others, so that in experiencing one, we experience all the elements in one degree or another.

In addition, the experiences of our life in God don't just happen to us. They are the effects (and sometimes the causes and motivations) of ongoing action. For example, spiritual knowledge is seldom infused by a mystical experience. Spiritual knowledge comes through reading, prayer, living God's will. Such knowledge is also love, involves purification and achieves union. Love that seeks always the will of the Beloved requires knowledge of the Beloved. In other words, all four elements occur simultaneously in the ongoing practice of spirituality that endeavors to incarnate one's desire for and openness to God in one's daily life.

Prayer in this context is a deliberate stepping back to look at how this process is in fact unfolding in one's life. It looks backward and forward by examining the present moment. What has brought me here? What is *here*? Where is *here* leading me?

Those who pray regularly—with only the rarest exceptions—stress the need to get away from one's ordinary circumstances. They say it is very important to change one's geography in order to enter the geography of the soul. My own experience confirms this conviction. Saint Francis, who told his brothers that they carry their cell with them, also wrote a Rule for Hermitages and entered places of solitude. None of us is so focused and disciplined that he or she doesn't need extra help from time to time to replenish the wells of the spirit by leaving the desert of one's spiritual aridity and going physically to a place where hidden spiritual water is abundant.

But where is that place of water? Sometimes, as in so much spiritual literature, it is the place of paradox: in the desert is water, in the full well is the empty cistern. So perhaps the desert we are fleeing in order to be filled up again is the place of filling. As T. S. Eliot says in *Four Quartets,* "We shall not cease from exploration, / And the end of all our exploring / Will be to arrive where we started / And know the place for the first time."[1]

A story in Martin Buber's *Tales of the Hasidim* further illustrates this point:

Rabbi Bunam used to tell young men who came to him for the first time the story of Rabbi Eisik, son of Rabbi Yekel in Cracow. After many years of great poverty which had never shaken his faith in God, he dreamed someone bade him look for a treasure in Prague, under the bridge which leads to the King's palace. When the dream recurred a third time, Rabbi Eisik prepared for the journey and set out for Prague. But the bridge was guarded day and night and he did not dare to start digging. Nevertheless he went to the bridge every morning and kept walking around it until evening.

Finally the captain of the guards, who had been watching him, asked in a kindly way whether he was looking for something or waiting for somebody. Rabbi Eisik told him of the dream which had brought him here from a faraway country. The captain laughed: "And so to please the dream, you poor fellow wore out your shoes to come here! As for having faith in dreams, if I had had it, I should have had to get going when a dream once told me to go to Cracow and dig for treasure under the stove in the room of a Jew—Eisik, son of Yekel, that was the name! Eisik, son of Yekel! I can just imagine what it would be like, how I should have to try every house over there, where one half of the Jews are named Eisik, and the other half Yekel!" And he laughed again. Rabbi Eisik bowed, traveled home, dug up the treasure from under the stove, and built the House of Prayer which is called "Reb Eisik's Shul."

"Take this story to heart," Rabbi Bunam used to add, "and make what it says your own: there is something you cannot find anywhere in the world, not even at the zaddik's, and there, is nevertheless, a place where you can find it."[2]

In this story I see the same cyclic pattern as in the above quote from T. S. Eliot: What we are looking for is close to home, even within us, but we need to leave to know it or appreciate it.

For example, when I was a boy of twelve, I would some evenings go over to the convent of Franciscan sisters and sit with them in the backyard of the convent. They were almost other-worldly beings to me with their white, nursing-sister habits with all those hidden, mysterious pockets, and the ever-present leather scabbard that held always a matching pen and pencil and hung from the belt-like Franciscan cord that circled their waists. And what was beneath those starched, brittle-looking wimples? Were their heads shaved? And did it chafe them to wear such tight-fitting veils?

They lived in a world of prayer and intimacy with God, and I wondered if they actually heard God and did God appear to them as they meditated in the quiet of their small chapel?

The image of myself sitting in the back yard of the convent listening to Sisters Jean and Damascene, Limbania and Josephine and Elisa, remains with me, but I had to leave Gallup to discover the image continued deep within. Each time I am moved to prayer, I am trying to recapture the scene of hearing the nuns read passages from Thomas Merton's *The Seven Storey Mountain* when I was a twelve-year-old boy. Surrounding Merton's book are all those "holy" feelings I experienced talking with the nuns, serving as altar boy for their 6:30 Mass every morning, driving their white 1949 Ford for Sister Damascene as she made home visits to the sick and aged among the mostly poor Mexican/Croatian/Italian/Indian population north of the Santa Fe Railroad tracks.

In the midst of my budding adolescence, those evenings on the nuns' back steps, those mornings in their chapel, those visits to the sick, were oases of prayer, adventure, quest for hidden treasure, magic, initiation, rites of passage, sacred spaces, ceremonies, pilgrimages.

Another scene: I am walking from the Piazza of St. Clare up a long winding street to St. Anthony's Hospice in Assisi. It is night. A bus has transported me to this spur of Mount Subasio from the Assisi train station on the plain below, where the train halts momentarily at St. Mary of the Angels, a modern suburb of the medieval city of Assisi. I have traveled via Rome from Cincinnati the day before. As I make my way into the heart of Assisi to St. Anthony's Hospice, I am also entering the nuns' backyard, a boy again.

I will spend many summers in Assisi, leading pilgrims back to that stone building on Second Street in Gallup, for what they will discover in Assisi is what I discovered in the company of those Franciscan sisters so many years before: a desire, a call to find what those sisters found in what Saint Francis and Saint Clare found. And each attempt to discover that hidden treasure moves the heart toward silence and solitude.

NOTES

[1] T. S. Eliot, *Collected Poems 1909–1962* (New York: Harcourt, Brace and World, Inc., 1970), p. 208.
[2] Martin Buber, *Tales of the Hasidim: The Later Masters* (New York: Schocken Books, 1948), p. 3.

Pilgrimage

Two texts sustain me on life's pilgrimage. The first is from the Bible, 1 Kings 19. The prophet Elijah, fleeing from the wrath of Jezebel, ventures a day's journey into the wilderness where he sits down under a broom tree. Exhausted, he asks the Lord to let him die.

> Suddenly an angel touched him and said to him, "Get up and eat." He looked, and there at his head was a cake baked on hot stones, and a jar of water. He ate and drank, and lay down again. The angel of the LORD came a second time, touched him, and said, "Get up and eat, otherwise the journey will be too much for you." He got up, and ate and drank; then he went in the strength of that food forty days and forty nights to Horeb the mount of God. (1 Kings 19:5–8)

In this text there is an angel. There is the mystical number forty. There is mysterious food and drink without which the prophet's journey to the mount of God would be too great for him. These elements symbolize for me the dynamic of pilgrimage. To arrive at that place within one must have reached that extremity of flight or fear or defeat that lies down in the wilderness and cannot go on, that wishes only to die. Then some "angel" of hope offers food and drink that restores the soul—a friend's encouragement, a book perhaps, a therapist's or spiritual director's listening soul, a visitation of the Spirit of God, unbidden and surprising—and one gets up and proceeds to God's mountain in the strength of the "angel's food" internalized as renewed faith and hope.

The second text follows immediately upon the first in 1 Kings and relates what happens to Elijah when he finally reaches God's mountain.

> At that place he came to a cave, and spent the night there. Then the word of the LORD came to him, saying to him, "Go out and stand on the mountain before the

Lord, for the LORD is about to pass by." Now there was a great wind, so strong that it was splitting mountains and breaking rocks in pieces before the LORD, but the LORD was not in the wind; and after the wind an earthquake, but the LORD was not in the earthquake; and after the earthquake a fire, but the LORD was not in the fire; and after the fire a sound of sheer silence. When Elijah heard it, he wrapped his face in his mantle and went out and stood at the entrance of the cave. (1 Kings 19:9–13)

The sound of sheer silence is heard inside the cave of the soul where God's mountain is. To enter the soul is to climb God's mountain within in search of the cave where God's sheer silence is heard. And this entering the cave is not a concentration of the mind. It is a handing over of the whole self, an embrace and caring for the leper, the marginal, the poor, as did Saint Francis. For the Franciscan, God dwells in the poorest person. It may seem an illogical jump to move from "a sound of pure silence" to the poor and marginal of the earth. But that jump is precisely the consequence of any movement of the soul to God. In the mystical world one does not attain union with God solely by meditation on God, but by living one's life in response to God's own self-giving. God sent the Son to show us how to live and only the Son can reveal the Father. Jesus is the gift of God. Our union with God is effected by returning that gift through the gradual transformation of our own life into the image of Jesus Christ. Jesus' life becomes the template of how one contemplates God.

For the Franciscan the events of the life of Christ become the focus of the mind's meditation. But not for the sake of mental consolation and peace. Meditation on the events of Christ's life move the soul to respond with affective love, with praise and gratitude, and above all, with a corresponding action in one's life—even in spiritual darkness and what is called in the apophatic tradition, the void. For all is not sweetness and light in meditation on the life of Christ. Sometimes there is nothing, no feeling, no images, no consolation. This experience of the void is what Saint Francis calls non-appropriation or detachment, particularly detachment from a self-centered looking for and clinging to God. It is the rejection of *appropriato*, appropriation to oneself of that which is gift of God, the great Almsgiver.

We enter silence and solitude; we arrive at detachment from the desire for visions and voices; we carry with us this detachment, this void within, wherever we go. And out of this void, in this detachment, we begin to converse with Jesus and Mary, dialogue with the voices of the Gospels, see the Bridegroom, the Lover, the Resurrected Christ, the Cosmic Christ, the Christ of the Gospels, the Christ of Paul, the Christ of Revelation. The void is the form that the ego tried in vain to elicit by techniques and prayers and longing. In the letting go is the void; in the void is that which was let go of; formless void becomes the form of the union longed for and released.

The Mysticism of the
Historical Event

The Franciscan way of prayer that I was introduced to as a high school seminarian has been called by Franciscan scholar Ewert Cousins the mysticism of the historical event. An apt description of how we were taught to pray. This way of prayer consists of meditating on a scene from the Bible, placing yourself in the scene, then letting the sacred action unfolding there reveal its meaning to you. And because you are in prayer, silent and open to God's word, this way of meditating is not just an intellectual exercise whereby you get some insight or new knowledge. Grace is given. You are moved and empowered to put into practice in your daily life the lesson or meaning or direction you have received in prayer. What you receive in a degree of change, in discernment, in charity, in virtue and so on as a result of your meditation is the enduring dimension of prayer. You take with you what has been given in prayer.

What makes prayer ongoing is the gradual transformation of the one who prays. That transformation, in turn, enables you to enter again and again into prayer with its silence and solitude and withdrawal from the busyness of your ordinary occupations and preoccupations.

What this transformation is depends on who the prayer is and on what needs transforming. Transformation is an individual experience, yet not so unique that certain patterns and dynamics cannot be discerned. A novice prayer, for example, most often experiences how difficult it is to settle down, be silent, listen. And the most significant transformation at this time concerns the transforming of one's inner noise into a space of silent listening. A more mature prayer may come to realize how selfish his or her silence and solitude has become. It needs to be peopled with others who are held in holy silence and prayed for or at least included like silent sentinels of one's own prayer. The transformation here is from self-centeredness to the charity of inclusion and the expansion of one's inner world. Here what is characteristic of your prayer are the loved ones (and perhaps even enemies) you carry into and out of prayer.

The most advanced prayers speak of needing no scenes to meditate on, no sacred word(s) to lead them into prayer, no images, no meaning or purpose. They simply enter into their own inner silence and listen. At times they don't even listen. They are simply there: no expectations, no purposes, no action at all. This, they say, is for them the truest, most trusted prayer. It is what they go into prayer for: to simply be.

It is important to understand that the examples I've given above are not stages you move through like walking up a ladder toward some perfect state. They are recursive, in the sense that you move back and forth from one kind of prayer to another at different times. Even the most experienced prayer may feel the need for words and images, and the novice may experience the imageless prayer of total silence. In other words, prayer is not a contest or competition to achieve some state or stage of perfection. Prayer is rather surrendering to whatever the time of prayer gives you— which could be no more than a headache, for not every entering upon prayer is made under the most auspicious circumstances. Sometimes one is so preoccupied and stressed that prayer time becomes a time to sleep and rest or to try to regain equilibrium by taking long walks in the woods or sitting numb before the fireplace and letting the crackling flames work their own magic. And that, too, is a transforming experience.

In the end, then, what is lasting is what you become because you pray and tend to your inner life with God. And what you become draws you back into prayer for further growth and transformation. Gradually, the mysticism of the historical event becomes the mysticism of the event your own life in God is. You become the event you only witnessed at the beginning of your prayer life. You realize God is working in and through you just as God worked in and through Moses and Mohammed and Jesus and your most admired saint. You become a witness to the transforming power of prayer.

PART FOUR:

The Door to the Holy Grail

Surrendering to Now

I am sitting in the kitchen of a Franciscan retreat house on Cape Cod. It is early morning, the second week of May; and I am still reeling from the ending of the school year and all the last minute details attended to before leaving for retreat. This is the beginning of my second full day here, and already I'm anxious because nothing seems to be happening. I stress *seems* because I realize that last night was the first good night's sleep I've had in a long time. And I like the silence.

I am the only one here in this beautiful old house, a restored 1920s summer home that belonged to someone obviously affluent. I accept it as gift; I don't question how it's consonant with Franciscan poverty or why I'm here instead of at some poor, austere setting. I am here; God is here. The morning is good, the coffee is, too.

I have written these personal reflections in order to demystify prayer. They sound, I hope, like someone's first couple of days on vacation. The gradual unwinding, the letting go of the need to judge and justify, the beginnings of observation, of noticing tangible things like the tenor of the morning, the taste of coffee, the sun on the bay, the fishing boats still and expectant, looking almost afraid to rock or move lest they betray their presence to the unseen fish, the feeling that something more should be happening. Instead, there is only the silence, the absence of obligation, of schedules, of people to assuage or assure or simply attend to. I am doing nothing; I am trying not to be disturbed or anxious about that.

So far I've not even attended to God. I'm confident God will find me and is quite content that I am content, like the friends and confreres who've seen me off to this retreat, who've wished me well, who are praying for me. If I work too hard at God-stuff just now, I'm beginning to do the same thing I'd hoped to get away from by coming here: over-compensating for my lack of prayerfulness by cramming prayer into intense little packets of time, feeling guilty because I don't attend to God as much as I should, trying to do everything myself instead of giving God credit for being as attentive to me as I try to be to God. I'm letting go of all that *should* stuff: I *should* do this. I *should* be there. I *should* feel this or that, or think this or that.

I look out the window and see an image of me in the fisherman sitting on the still water waiting. If anything comes along that's interested in his bait, he's ready for it. He's just there, hook in the water, waiting. I'm just here, words falling onto the page, waiting for something to pull the words under like a bobber, take them to a deeper level, struggle with me over them, come up beautiful and flashing in the morning sun, moving me to awe and thanksgiving and praise for the Creator of such a catch. But I can't make that happen. All I can do is sit here waiting with words or bait or silence or openness or contrition or whatever stance I take before the mystery of all that I cannot control, all that is pure gift, there for those who wait in humility and receptivity.

I have not made my bed nor said Mass yet. I've not even splashed my face with water or combed my hair. I'm just sitting here writing, not worrying about when I'll make my bed, when I'll say Mass. I'll do it when I run out of words, when I tire of just sitting and waiting for words that no longer come. I'll make my own schedule.

A completely personal and even eccentric schedule is one of the main differences between a private, hermit-like prayer experience and a communal retreat. As soon as two or three gather together, there is need for some kind of accommodation, flexibility, scheduling of times and places for gathering, sharing, eating, sleeping, in short, all of those activities that involve awareness of and accommodation to the needs of others. There is much consolation, support, community, even communion in a shared, communal retreat. There is solitude, silence, individuality and even whimsy in a private, "unstructured" time of prayer.

"Unstructured" with quotation marks because even the most individualistic, or eccentric of private retreats will find its own structure or, perhaps more accurately, its own rhythm. The day will begin to unfold according to the heart's deepest needs, those needs that moved me to enter this kind of retreat in the first place: the need to get away from routine or responsibilities or noise or people and enter a more silent, receptive space where I can hear something other than the voices of my ordinary world. The need to get away from it all, yes, but also the need to hear God, to know God more intimately, or at least to sit in silence and expectation like a Cape Cod fisherman who won't know if there's any fish in the bay if he doesn't at least put a hook in the water and wait. And even if nothing bites, something happens. He's gone out fishing, he's seen the sun rise over the placid water, he's contemplated early morning, he's learned to wait in silent expectation. Sooner or later, if not today or tomorrow, if not this week, then someday, some week, it will happen—that tug on the line, that unseen pull that evidences something underwater has come calling.

The faith of one who prays is the same: sooner or later, something will happen, something unseen, something numinous, that may be tangible only in the good effect it has on me. And once that happens, I am drawn back into solitude again and again. Prayer then becomes a pattern of my living, like going on vacation or celebrating holidays or visiting loved ones. In fact, a prayer-retreat is another kind of vacation, a celebration of holy-days, a visiting of a Loved One. It partakes in the dynamic of all three because grace builds on nature, as Saint Thomas Aquinas wisely observed. Grace is not something apart from what we are and do naturally; it is an extension of the natural, a stretching of the natural, a lifting up of the natural. Grace enhances all that I am and do; grace is the gift of God that charges everything within and without with God's glory. In the words of the poet Gerard Manley Hopkins, grace enables me to experience and see that "the world is charged with the glory of God."[1]

And this is where this morning's word-meditation has brought me. It is 9:20. I sat down at 7:00. I've been unaware of the time till now. I've all the time in the world to make my bed, to say Mass, to walk, to do whatever needs doing before I sit down to eat lunch. I'm beginning to enter into that unawareness of time that is the first step in moving from the active to the contemplative life, from the workaday world to the world of solitude and prayer. To enter into the eternal is to stop counting minutes and hours and surrender to the now.

NOTES

[1] Gerard Manley Hopkins, *Poems and Prose* (New York: Penguin Books, 1985), p. 27.

A Gong

Thich Nhat Hanh recounts an exchange with an American Catholic priest:

> ". . . I see the value of mindfulness practice. I have tasted the joy, peace, and happiness of it. I have enjoyed the bells, the walking, the tea meditation, and the silent meals. But how can I continue to practice when I get back to my church?"
>
> I asked him, "Is there a bell in your church?"
>
> He said, "Yes."
>
> "Do you ring the bell?"
>
> "Yes."
>
> "Then please ring your bell as a bell of mindfulness calling you back to your true home. . . . Our true home is the present moment, the miracle is not to walk on water. The miracle is to walk on the green earth in the present moment."[1]

Here at the Franciscan Retreat House on Cape Cod there is a large gong, about the size of a small car tire, in the glassed-in porch that fronts the canal. Someone brought it from Bali as a gift to the friars. It hangs in a wooden frame that looks like the headboard of a child's bed. It is suspended on a gold-colored cord, and its ringer is a wooden-handled round mallet whose head is wrapped in cloth enclosed in a fretwork of heavy string. The center of the gong has a raised bronze "eye" that one strikes to produce a sound that resonates more like a sustained hum than a bell's ring. I strike this gong in the morning when I begin prayer and again in the evening just before supper when I am ending my day of meditation and prayer. This "Om-sounding" hum leads me into and out of a holy space. If, for any reason, I leave the friary during the day, I strike the gong to remind me that I am moving from something interior to the external world. I strike it again when I return. The gong comforts me, reminds me, marks entrances and exits, but above all, transports me to the plane of prayer.

What I find most interesting about this gong is how I have chosen to make it an important part of this week of prayer and reflection. What is it about bells and gongs, wooden sound-boxes and drawn or plucked strings that invite us to enter their resonance, their vibration as into another dimension? Something happens inside me each time I strike the gong. This morning I've struck it often, simply because on this third day of retreat I am beginning to be distracted by everything that is waiting for me to attend to it when I return home. I've begun, too, to wonder how I am going to finish this book, bring some kind of closure to my father's estate, find time to work more intensely, preach two retreats in the midst of trying to write and on and on.

It's time for big-time gong striking. I need to surrender all of that, I need to remember that I am in the presence of God, who alone can anoint everything I do and give it life and purpose and sanctity. The gong begins to serve as a weapon against distraction, a call to focus again, to come back onto the plane of prayer. In fact, I may begin to strike the gong twice, once forcefully to drive out distractions, and again more lightly to welcome me back to prayer.

Now this is the sort of action that can become compulsively repetitive, something the person given to using external objects as foci of prayer needs to be aware of. Any prayer activity, or activity associated with prayer that becomes needlessly repetitive and frenetic, is an invitation to superficiality and the substitution of external activity for inner centering and peace of heart. I am reminded of Jesus' words, "When you are praying, do not heap up empty phrases as the Gentiles do; for they think they will be heard because of many words. Do not be like them, for your Father knows what you need before you ask him" (Matthew 6:7–9). And then Jesus goes on to give the disciples the Lord's Prayer as the model of their prayer.

What I have said here is in no way intended to denigrate repetitive prayers, like mantras, like the Rosary or the repetition of the Jesus Prayer, "Lord Jesus Christ, Savior, Son of the Living God, have mercy on me, a sinner." I am simply pointing out that repetition can become compulsion instead of the reverent repetition of words or ringing of bells that massages the mind, coun-teracts the chaotic speed of thoughts and feelings by inviting us to enter another rhythm or sound.

That being said, I return to this place, this sound of the gong. What does it do for me specifically? Like the old Angelus prayer that people would recite when they heard the church bells ring-ing three, followed by three, followed by three and then rung continuously for a couple of minutes, the gong calls me back to mindfulness of God. In fact, I have begun to strike the gong at noon after the manner of the Angelus to remind me of my Catholic Christian belief in the Incarnation. This prayer that goes back to the Middle Ages, goes like this: The bell is struck three times during which is recited, "The Angel of the Lord de-clared unto Mary, and she conceived of the Holy Spirit. Hail Mary, full of grace, the Lord is with thee, blessed art thou among women, and blessed is the fruit of thy womb, Jesus. Holy Mary, Mother of God, pray for us sinners now and at the hour of our death. Amen." The bell is then struck three more times, during which is recited, "Behold the handmaid of the Lord. Be it done to me according to thy word." And again the Hail Mary is recited, followed by three more rings during which is recited, "And the word was made flesh and dwelt among us," followed again by the Hail Mary. Then as the bell is rung uninterruptedly, the prayer says, "Pray for us, O Holy Mother of God, that we may be made worthy of the promises of Christ. Let us pray. Pour forth, we be-seech thee, O Lord, thy grace into our hearts, that we, to whom the Incarnation of thy Son was made known by the message of an Angel, may, by his Passion and Cross, be brought to the glory of his Resurrection. Through the same Christ our Lord. Amen. May the souls of the faithful departed, through the mercy of God, rest in peace. Amen." People would pause in their work, as in the famous painting *The Angelus* by Millet, and bow their heads and recite this formula of prayer. It was the Christian's way of re-calling and reverencing the central belief of Christianity, the Incarnation of God made known in the Annunciation by the Angel Gabriel, immortalized in so many paintings from the Middle Ages to the present day.

The Angelus is one of many formulas of prayer that are referred to in Catholicism as devotions. One need not, of course, recite the Angelus at the striking of the gong, the ringing of bells. But there may be some other prayer that comes automatically to one's lips, a mantra one has learned, one's own prayer composed to include the words that are central to one's own belief, or simply silence, itself a deep prayer when it becomes an openness to God. The point is that the external object, gong or bell, leads us inward, locates us again in the holy.

NOTES

[1] Thich Nhat Hanh, *Living Buddha, Living Christ* (New York: Riverhead Books, 1995), pp. 22–23.

Living the Mass

It is late morning. The Mass is ended; the Mass begins. For I bring with me from the celebration of Mass a conviction that I am to live the dynamic of the Mass throughout the rest of my day, a dynamic that goes like this:

Every Mass begins with an entrance antiphon, a passage from Holy Scripture that greets the celebrant as he processes to the altar. The entrance antiphon for Mass this morning, Monday, May 20, is this passage from the Acts of the Apostles: "You will receive power when the Holy Spirit comes upon you. You will be my witnesses to all the world, alleluia." Words of Jesus which I take not only into the Mass but into my whole day. These words of Jesus go before me, so to speak, as a light to the entrances of whatever portals I will pass through during the day.

The Mass then moves into a silent period of reflection on one's sins and failings in order to place them before God for God's forgiveness. This brief period of repentance ends with the ancient, *"Kyrie eleison, Christe eleison, Kyrie eleison,"* which today is said or sung in the vernacular, "Lord, have mercy, Christ, have mercy, Lord, have mercy." It is significant that this time of repentance is brief. To concentrate excessively on one's sins or failings or un-worthiness makes of prayer a time of self-preoccupation rather than a time of openness to God's forgiveness, God's unconditional love. I simply acknowledge my sins, ask God's forgiveness, then move on to giving praise and glory to God through the Gloria of the Mass, which follows immediately upon receiving God's forgiveness. "Glory to God in the highest and peace to his people on earth. Lord God, heavenly King, almighty God and Father, we worship you, we give you thanks, we praise you for your glory. Lord Jesus Christ, only Son of the Father, Lord God, Lamb of God, you take away the sin of the world: have mercy on us; you are seated at the right hand of the Father: receive our prayer. For you alone are the Holy One, you alone are the Lord, you alone are the Most High, Jesus Christ, with the Holy Spirit, in the glory of God the Father. Amen."

The Gloria is followed by a brief prayer to conclude this part of the Mass. The prayer for today is: "Lord, send the power of your Holy Spirit upon us that we may remain faithful and do your will in our daily lives."

Next follow the readings from Holy Scripture, two for week-days, three for Sundays and major feast days. One's prayer-life is often helped from day to day by some kind of reading from a sa-cred text followed by a short reflection.

The Mass then proceeds to the offering of the gifts of bread and wine, symbolic of God's gifts of nourishment to us that we have, in turn, transformed into bread and wine and that at the consecration of the Mass will be further transformed into the Body and Blood of Christ to be received by us in Communion, thereby uniting us in the most intimate, personal way with God, who through this sacrament gradually transforms us into a pure and living offering to God. We become the gifts we offer to God at the beginning of the Offertory.

It is this dynamic from offering to transubstantiation to com-munion that most dramatically models what should transpire when we enter into prayer. The whole purpose of prayer is union with God, and the dynamic of the Catholic Mass demonstrates how one such union is effected. For the Catholic, then, prayer is really a more intense living out of the Mass by finding a measure of solitude and silence every day in which to reflect upon what is already happening in one's life through participation in the Mass. Prayer is also a more intense preparation and thanksgiv-ing for the transformation that is being accomplished in us through the liturgical action of the Mass.

After Communion a brief antiphon is recited or sung. In today's Mass the antiphon is from the Gospel of John. "The Lord said: I will not leave you orphans. I will come back to you, and your hearts will rejoice, alleluia." The antiphon is followed by a brief closing prayer and a sending forth. The closing prayer for today's Mass is "Merciful Father, may these mysteries give us new purpose and bring us to a new life in you."

The celebration of daily Mass usually takes about a half hour, and for many Catholics the attendance at Mass *focuses* their day:

a day of repentance, for example, and a day for glorifying God, a day for offering one's own life and all of creation to God, a day for surrendering the self you brought with you to Mass to God's transforming love, a love that will return your life to you, purified, transformed, a day for embracing the life God is giving back to you, a day for reflecting on how you can offer your new life in God to others. The Mass always involves a sending forth to love more deeply and unconditionally as God loves you.

Prayer, too, involves a sending forth to live more charitably, compassionately in your own world. True prayer, I believe, is attainable by everyone willing to take prayer-time every day. And prayer effects an inner transformation, no matter what your religious roots are, just as true prayer will eventually embrace all of the elements of the Mass, either really or symbolically.

A Meditation

Rumpled sheets of silk. The sea-breeze, even with the sun full at noon, is cool as I stare out onto Buzzards Bay. It has been a cold spring, they say, and even as recently as last week when I arrived I had to wear a wool sweater and windbreaker. Now it is short-sleeve weather, and yet as I sit on the dock, the cool breeze makes me reach automatically for my jacket. It is silent here, silent enough to hear not just the calls but the wing-beats of the birds. I'm trying to shut out the fact that I am leaving this hermitage tomorrow (it's been a short ten days), but thoughts of New York City with its noise and frenetic pace assault my solitude. Can I find even there a space for prayer, short of a penthouse far above the traffic? The courtyard of the friary on Thompson Street in the Village shines on memory's screen, and peace settles over me.

I am back here on Cape Cod, the silence not disturbed just now even by wing beat or gull cry. A small sailboat slides silently across the middle of the canal, its red, yellow and green sail looking from here like a large butterfly wing. *Take this in,* I tell myself. *Be here now, not somewhere else. Be here where the boats lie idle, rock gently like hollow bobbers and what birds there are beat their wings far out in the canal.* A jet statics overhead, but I tune it out, wait for the silence that will quickly replace the jet's fading grumble. Like all the noise of our lives the jet's noise will leave silence behind. Wait. Enter the silence; don't let noise disturb you; it's the prelude to silence. At least *here* it is, and here is where I am, what I try to surrender to. The silence of feathers.

Suddenly, it is dark. A large rain cloud passes overhead. A long barge slides up the Cape Cod canal, where a short time ago the "butterfly wing" shone in the sun. An ominous black cloud. I don't like the looks, the feel of the atmosphere. I go to the car, turn on the radio. "A severe thunderstorm watch has been issued for Barnstable County and surrounding coastal areas. Hail, lightning and dangerous winds are possible. A 'watch' means that conditions are favorable for a thunderstorm. If you are within the sound of my voice, please monitor the weather in your area."

Boats are coming in. The silence now is eerie.

The Door to the Holy Grail

I have hanging over my bed a simple silk-screened print of Moses kneeling before the burning bush. Why is he kneeling? Who lit the bush? Why has he removed his shoes? The desire to know the answer to those three questions is the impetus for withdrawing for a while from the daily, physical world I hear and see and touch and taste and smell, the world I know the usual scientific explanation of, even though I may not turn to it. Is there anything else besides the usual tangible reality around me? Is there anything inside, beyond that reality? Is there anything I can do to know that numinous world, if in fact it exists?

It is in prayer that I begin to look beyond the immediate preoccupations of my life to the greater questions innate in the human heart. I find my own immortality in questions like, Who am I? Why am I here? Where am I going? What can I take with me? How long will I be there?

The answer to these questions are the desire of the self in solitude, and all the religions of the world give us answers. Our own answers, however, come from the heart of prayer. They may be the very answers of the religious tradition we've grown up with, but in the cell within, they become our own.

How do I get there? I know from so many who have gone before me. The great prophets and seers of the religions of our small planet tell us there's something "out there" that is heard and seen "in here," the center of the cell within. I desire to seek. But how do I enter? Where is the door? What is inside?

When Saint Francis speaks of the cell within and the soul as the hermit who dwells in it, he is not speaking of cell as a prison cell, but cell as the monk's cell, the hermit's cell. This cell within the body is not built by human hands, it is made by God. And it is good and beautiful. And in it lives the hermit I call my soul.

One such image, of a secret interior space holding a great treasure waiting to be discovered, is Stephen Spielberg's modern interpretation of the ancient grail legend, *Indiana Jones and the*

Last Crusade. When explored, his images help to illumine what happens in a life of prayer.

In the film the old knight who is found guarding the Holy Grail and who has been there in that secret cavern for almost eight hundred years, is an image of the one who will finally attain the place within which is the source of eternal life. In this case, the source is the cup that Christ drank from at the Last Supper. And Indiana, in order to save his own father who has been mortally wounded, uses the knowledge his father (a grail scholar) has passed on to him by way of his diary. The diary contains the way to the old knight and to the grail cup in these cryptic words: (1) The breath of God. Only the penitent man will pass. (2) The Word of God. Only in the footsteps of God will he proceed. (3) The path of God. Only in the leap from the lion's head will he prove his worth.

There are booby traps set to slay anyone who thinks he or she can march right into the place of the Holy Grail.

The penitent is the one who kneels before God and in kneeling avoids the revolving blade that severs the head of one who would come before God, head erect, self-sufficient and proud. The self-righteously upright person triggers the lever that releases the lethal blade.

Then there is a floor of inset stones, each with a letter of the alphabet which the seeker must walk upon to get to the other side. Most of the stones will give way and drop you into a deep crevasse to your own death. But Indiana Jones has his father's diary which reads, "Only in the footsteps of God will he proceed." Indiana reasons that he must step on the stones with the letters J, E, H, O, V, A, H, but errs in his first step and almost falls through because in Latin there is no "J." "J" is replaced by "I," which Jones concludes finally and passes successfully this further test.

Then he comes to a deep, seemingly uncrossable chasm. There is an opening into a cave on the other side of the canyon, but there is no way across. There is only the "leap of faith" written in his father's diary as the last step to be taken. And that, at last, is what Jones does. He simply walks out into the empty air of the canyon, and his foot rests firmly on an invisible bridge that was there all along. The empty space was an illusion, which only the faith to walk on air unmasked. And thus, Indiana Jones reaches the old knight and the grail.

Now, to some this may sound terribly corny, or at least like a nice story for an old-fashioned movie scenario. But for anyone who has actually tried to find the place within, the movie (corny or not) becomes a parable. You don't just stride naively into the place within. You need a guide, first of all (the "father" and his text). There will be obstacles and illusions, and most of all, the temptation to think you can go it alone, without the obeisance of the penitent person who knows that only in God's name will the passage be made, only in supernatural faith will the chasm be crossed. And then, as in the movie, when you finally arrive, there will be many cups to choose from. Which one is Christ's?

The antagonist in the movie secretly follows Indiana into the cave, not finding his own way but walking behind Indiana Jones, letting him do the work for him. The evil person goes immediately to the most beautiful gold and bejewelled cup as worthy to be the cup of eternal life. He thinks only of himself and how he will live forever if he drinks from this cup. He drinks to his own death. For as soon as he drinks, he ages and withers and is reduced to dust.

Indiana, thinking not of himself but of his dying father, chooses a simple, wooden cup because Christ was a poor carpenter, and this wooden cup must indeed be the Holy Grail. He drinks and does not die; he pours holy water from this cup onto his father's gunshot wound, and his father is immediately healed.

All of the elements we will encounter on the inner journey are here: the way in, the being in long enough to choose the grail, the coming-out "healed" and with the means of healing others.

The grail story is another image, a variation of the original grail story, which is itself an image of the search for God. Similarly, the cell/soul image of Saint Francis comes from Francis' journey from a subterranean prison cell as a prisoner of war to mountain-cave cells of freedom and solace where he finds a spring of water inside himself that re-orders his world of lepers and wars and that sustains him to joyfully follow the quest and enter into the grail, which for him is the literal gospel life of Christ.

While Francis' life was real, the quest to seek the grail is archetypal. It is a theme throughout the literature of the ages, such as in Cervantes's *Don Quixote de la Mancha*. The contemporary poet, Linda Gregg, puts the quest another way in a poem, replete with the biblical imagery of the desert, entitled, "My Father and God."

> He abandoned us every year, four daughters and a wife. Drove with gallons of water along both sides of the jeep to lie on his stomach at sunrise on sand and stone surrounded by rock and sand. To know distance and know the close-up. Because he believed it was near to God. The place nobody wanted. The parts of the world left alone. The flatness where things are broken down to the clearest form. He would say it was the simple he wanted. Sun coming up and shining first on the bottom of your feet as you are looking at flowers appearing out of sand. A lizard lying on a hot stone knowing the lightning wants to strike something. Knowing lightning has no mouth, no teeth, not even a stomach; but when it strikes, the lizard will race wriggling up to God's shining face, which is so bright that no one can see anything but the glare. The sun is always there or dark. Far off or close up. My father lived out where God could kill him. That is the way of real desire. . . .[1]

Real desire. The way of desire. Without desire we will not even begin the journey. The desire merely to start. A few moments, a glance, a thought. Aldous Huxley writes:

> We apprehend Him in the alternate voids and fullness of a cathedral; in the space that separates the salient features of a picture; in the living geometry of a flower, a seashell, an animal; in the pauses and intervals between the notes of music, in their difference of tones and sonority.[2]

Look for the pauses, the intervals, for that is often where the desire begins. God comes often as a surprise when we're listening to and looking at the intervals, the spaces within, where nothing great or intense seems to be happening and when our expectations are minimal, if they are there at all.

Grace happens more often than not when we are simply "going through the motions," so to speak: looking peacefully at a painting, listening to a piece of music we've heard hundreds of times before, praying a prayer we've been reciting since childhood, reading a sacred text we virtually know by heart.

So let us enter into a little time of prayer every day, a little time to look contemplatively at something at least once a week, a little time to "waste" time for a few minutes in the morning, at lunch break, in the evening. And it really can be just a few minutes; because if you put in those few minutes, they will grow into a way of seeing, a heart that has learned to slow down, a soul that desires to go in and be in the presence of its Creator, to return to the sacred ground of its making, a heart that will reenact the dynamic of desire that Dante portrays in the *Convivio*.

> The greatest desire of each thing, given first by nature, is to return to its beginning. And since God is the beginning of our souls and maker of those similar to himself (as is written: "Let us make man in our image and likeness"), the soul desires above all to return to him. And like the pilgrim who travels on a road on which he has never been, who thinks that every house he sees from a distance is the inn, and finding that it is not, redirects his belief to the next, and thus from house to house, until he comes to the inn; so our soul, as soon as it enters on the new and never before traveled path of this life, straightens its eyes to the terminus of its highest good . . . and then, whatever thing it sees that seems to have some good in it, the soul believes that it is the terminus. And because the soul's knowledge is at first imperfect, because it is neither expert nor learned, small goods seem to it to be big goods, and so from these it begins at first to desire. So we see children desire above all an apple; and then, proceeding further, a little bird; and then, further still, beautiful clothing; and then a horse; and then a lady; and then not great riches; and then great riches; and then more. And this happens because in none of these

things does the soul find what it is looking for, and it
believes that it will find it further on.[3]

Another image of the quest of the Holy Grail. Another instance
of not realizing that the cell I am going toward is really within
me all along.

NOTES

[1] Linda Gregg, *The Sacraments of Desire* (St. Paul, Minn.: Graywolf Press, 1991),
p. 14.
[2] Quoted in *The Quiet Eye, A Way of Looking at Pictures,* selected and introduced
by Sylvia Shaw Judson (Chicago: Henry Regnery Company, 1954), p. 5.
[3] Dante Alighieri, *Convivio,* 4.12.14–16, in Teodolinda Barolini, *The Undivine
Comedy: Detheologizing Dante* (Princeton, N.J.: Princeton University Press,
1992), p. 100.

Obstacles

I cannot by mere desire make God present in my life. But my desire for God can and does lead to action and resolution to remove from my life everything that would prevent me from hearing and seeing the living God, should God choose to reveal himself to me. The work of the spiritual life is mainly in removing obstacles to my ongoing desire to live in and for God. All the rest is the gift of God, who may or may not give me a felt experience of God's immanence in my life. In other words, as in any relationship I cannot control how much love will come from the other; I can only try to make myself worthy of whatever love the other returns.

But here there is need of caution and common sense. For in removing obstacles and trying to make myself worthy, I can think that I'm doing too much work or become discouraged if God does not respond as I anticipated. I may not realize at this point that removing obstacles and trying to be worthy is itself God's work. And this, too, is proof of God's presence to me: that I keep trying to remove obstacles, trying to be worthy (as impossible as that is). God is in my trying, as God is in my desire for God. I come to a point of seeing that if I could remove all obstacles, could be totally worthy, then my own pride and self-sufficiency would be my God. I work, therefore, knowing I will remove only what God allows me to remove to be closer to God, my Beloved.

Some obstacles God removes without my working at it to show me that even the areas where I think *I* need to do everything, even there God grants gifts, pure grace, before I ask for it or work at it. And still I work: trying to remove what obstacles I can, obstacles to my desire to be united with the Beloved. And that ongoing effort makes me more open to the divine within me and around me.

The classic obstacles to union with the Beloved are the so-called seven capital sins. They are called "capital" because they are the source of other sins. Following Saint John Cassian and

Saint Gregory the Great, the Catholic Church names these sins: pride, avarice, envy, wrath, lust, gluttony and sloth or acedia. If any of these sins control my life, then my desire for God is diminished by a counter-valence in my life.

How I work at removing these obstacles has much to do with who I am, with understanding myself and whether I should attack them directly, indirectly or not attack them at all, but rather concentrate on the opposite virtue. This is where the helping discernment of a spiritual guide can be invaluable. I may, for example, so violently try to rid myself of some sin that I replace one violence for another, one addiction for another, one compulsive form of behavior with another. I may need instead, to be more positive: to try to embrace the opposite virtue to my sin, thus letting the sin be transformed by its opposite virtue. For example, instead of violently trying to wrench lust out of my life, thereby becoming more preoccupied with the lust I'm trying to overcome, I may need instead to renounce all that negative energy and embrace charity as a pattern of action. Each time I am tempted by lust, I turn my attention to charity, to reaching out to someone difficult to love, someone in need. And each time I fail and fall into the sin of lust, instead of becoming discouraged or allowing myself to sink into self-hatred or a poor self-image, I simply ask God's forgiveness and turn again to developing my desire for God by trying to love those God has asked me to love: the poor, the outcasts, the marginal, the unloved, the unwanted of the earth.

Charity can transform lust into desire for God. Most of us learn this the hard way; some are fortunate enough to have a spiritual guide who discerns with them the best way for them as individuals to remove their particular obstacles to union with God. Without a guide I may not see that my biggest obstacle is trying too hard to remove obstacles, or that embracing the opposite virtue can be counterproductive if it involves a repression of the counter drive rather than an avoidance of sin. To use the example of lust again, if my embrace of charity is more a denial of my own sexuality than an avoidance of sin, then I am simply driving underground a strong libidinal drive, and that is unhealthy and can result in bizarre behavior deriving from my repressed sexuality.

Sexuality needs to be acknowledged as good because it is given by God; it needs to be embraced and transformed by supernatural love into a positive force in my life. A spiritual guide helps us discern whether what we are doing to remove obstacles is destructive denial or constructive transformation.

Now, having written the above rather convoluted material makes me uncomfortable. For while some do well working at obstacles in their spiritual life and advance steadily toward deeper love of God, others reading this are already becoming agitated, worried whether or not they are working hard enough, or working at the right obstacles. They become scrupulous, so obsessive-compulsive in their response to removing obstacles, that God gets lost in the equation.

As a spiritual director, I know that this is the wrong tack for these personalities. They need to forget obstacles, concentrate instead on God's love, on how much God loves them, on how little God is concerned with the minutiae they worry about. They need prayerful reflection on Scripture passages and parables that counteract the obsessive-compulsive need to work themselves to a frazzle about how much or how hard they are working. Jesus' consoling words, for example, "Do not let your hearts be troubled. . . . In my Father's house there are many dwelling places" (John 14:1–2). Or, "Come to me, all you that are weary and are carrying heavy burdens, and I will give you rest" (Matthew 11:28).

Or a parable of Jesus like the Laborers in the Vineyard:

> For the kingdom of heaven is like a landowner who went out early in the morning to hire laborers for this vineyard. After agreeing with the laborers for the usual daily wage, he sent them into his vineyard. When he went out about nine o'clock, he saw others standing idle in the marketplace; and he said to them, "You also go into the vineyard, and I will pay you whatever is right." So they went. When he went out again about noon and about three o'clock, he did the same. And about five o'clock he went out and found others standing around; and he said to them, "Why are you standing here idle all day?" They said to him, "Because no one has hired us." He said to them, "You also go into the vineyard." When the time came, the owner of the vineyard said to his manager, "Call the laborers and give them their pay, beginning with the

last and then going to the first." When those hired about five o'clock came, each of them received the usual daily wage. Now when the first came, they thought they would receive more; but each of them also received the usual daily wage. And when they received it, they grumbled against the landowner, saying, "These last worked only one hour, and you have made them equal to us who have borne the burden of the day and the scorching heat." But he replied to one of them, "Friend, I am doing you no wrong; did you not agree with me for the usual daily wage? Take what belongs to you and go; I choose to give to this last the same as I give to you. Am I not allowed to do what I choose with what belongs to me? Or are you envious because I am generous? So the last will be first, and the first will be last." (Matthew 20:1–15)

God does not operate with strict legalistic justice. God is merciful and compassionate. God will do what God will do. Ours is simply to return God's love, respond to his invitation, to emulate God's love and mercy by showing mercy and compassion to ourselves, first of all, then to all others who come our way—all the while putting God first in our attention, adoring and loving God with our whole mind and heart and soul.

I cannot focus on two things simultaneously. Therefore if whatever I am doing to grow closer to God is making me anxious and preoccupied with my own doing rather than with God, it is better to forget what *I* am doing and focus on God for whom I do all things. That focus will in itself work what I am frenetically trying to do by my own efforts.

The Showings

Sometimes it is an intuition that everything is slipping out from beneath me that impels me toward entering into prayer as a step backward, taken to find some solid ground to stand on.

This does not mean that prayer is an escape but that I pray in order to find the ground on which to take my stand again, face whatever problems and difficulties or conflicts are besieging me. From this point of view prayer *is* like a retreat on a battlefield, but only a temporary retreat to regroup and advance again. In the last poem of his last volume of poetry, *In the Clearing,* Robert Frost penned these lines:

> I see in nature no defeat
> In one tree's overthrow,
> Nor for myself in my retreat
> For yet another blow.[1]

Here retreat is not an escape or denial or hiding. Here retreat is finding one's center again in order to face life's reversals.

Some years ago, a few days after the terrorist attack on the TWA counter in Rome's Leonardo da Vinci Airport, I was walking through the terminal to catch an Alitalia flight back to New York. There were people rushing about in fear and anger and impatience, people anxiously waiting for flights missed when the attack occurred, policemen and soldiers patrolling, machine guns on their shoulder, menacing dogs stalking at their side.

I was moving through the crush of this crowd of pushing, noisy, frustrated travelers, when I saw a woman sitting on her suitcase in the middle of the floor, her nose in a book, totally oblivious to those around her. I couldn't resist approaching the peaceful figure and asking almost impertinently what book it was that so engaged her attention in the midst of the evident chaos around her. She turned a serene face to me and said in impeccable English, "I'm reading *The Showings* of Julian of Norwich; I am meditating on her words which matter the way all this hustle and bustle does not."This incident is the most dramatic image of concentration that I've encountered. Whatever it was that the woman was doing, *that* is what it means to carry your cell with you. She was able to enter it, even in the midst of the chaotic aftermath of the machine-gunning of the TWA counter in the Rome airport. She was obviously not going to sit there forever, but the time she spent inside the words of the medieval anchoress and mystic Julian of Norwich would make it possible for her to put everything in perspective, rise calmly and, lifting her suitcase, face whatever the rest of her day would bring. She had found a way to shut out everything around her and enter into her secret center.

NOTES

[1] Robert Frost, *The Poetry of Robert Frost*, p. 470.

The Chair

Y ou sit in this chair. You let yourself feel the weight of your sitting—the weight of your life pressing into the strong, safe chair. Your mother's chair, your father's—antique with ancestors. It held them; it will hold you. You begin to feel one with the chair and all who've sat here. There is a sense of pulling down and in, toward some source you didn't know you had it in you to draw from. And simultaneously with this inward/downward movement is the sense the chair is getting lighter or you are, and both of you are rising, floating in the air.

You remember that you have kissed in this chair, collapsed in grief here, rocked a child in your arms in this chair, watched wars begin and end from this chair. You have peeled potatoes here, your colander resting in your aproned lap. You have read in this chair, sipped wine, smoked your pipe or cigar or stopped smoking here. You have laughed and worried, cried and shouted for joy here. You have prayed in this chair. You have lived your life in and around this chair; you may die here. It is holy. It is an altar you can move anywhere in the house or outside the house. You can sit in this chair and not feel removed but connected to your life, your loves, your God.

Blessing the Animals

The first Sunday of October. We're blessing the animals in style. It's the Sunday after the Feast of Saint Francis, and I am processing with another friar down the aisle of the Cathedral of St. John the Divine in New York City. My heart pounds as I hear the howling of wolves over the public address system and see the shifting colored lights play over the gothic arches and ceiling and across hundreds of people with their dogs and cats and gerbils, their birds and lizards and snakes. The animals are strangely quiet, looking and listening as the Paul Winter Consort beats out African rhythms, and dancers representing different animals cavort down the aisle after us and then dance in the sanctuary. There are Episcopal and Roman Catholic priests here, rabbis and Buddhist monks and ministers of many Christian denominations. There is a cross section of New York City sitting in the pews with their animals and their prayers for safety and blessing for all the animal kingdom.

The procession into the cathedral, like the service itself and the blessing of the animals, is full of the drama of grand opera, even to the blessing of an elephant who seems to have strayed distractedly from the stage of *Aida*. There is the sound of humpback whales broadcast through the loud speakers at the Offertory. And after the service outside on the cathedral grounds there is piping and miming and individual blessings for thousands of pets offered in faith and hope to the waiting hands of bishops and priests and ministers.

It may not look like a time of deep prayer, but it is. For here there is praise and waiting for the moment of blessing to descend on a loved creature. There is prayer for the animals, there is reflection on what the animal kingdom means to us, what we have done or failed to do to live in harmony with animals and all of nature. There is silence—which astounds me—at the sacred moments of the service. How can all these thousands of animals be silent? One feels the presence of Saint Francis—the animals are listening.

The Blessing of the Animals at St. John the Divine is one of the most famous in America. Surely it is spectacular. It lasts from 11:00 A.M. till almost 1:30. It seems but a blinking of an eye, for we have all been worshiping with the animals we love. We imagine Saint Francis talking to the animals as he preached to the birds of Umbria, tamed the Wolf of Gubbio, talked to Sister Pheasant and Brother Lamb, Sister Lark and to his brother, the raven who kept him company on Mount LaVerna where he received the sacred stigmata. We've been making a nature retreat in a large city cathedral; we've made present what we thought we had to go out into the country to experience.

All of nature is as close as the plant on your windowsill, the dog or cat asleep on the couch. One of God's creatures cared for is all of God's creatures loved. One dog or cat blessed is all pets blessed. We have retreated into the space of a magnificent cathedral and transformed it into a giant lair. We have spent two and a half hours in prayer with all of God's creatures.

Centering

People are different. Some are focused and centered by what is outside them: a chair, a child, an icon, a sunset or waterfall, a ceremony or ritual. Others are centered by moving inward, by finding within a place and space of quiet, light and peace.

As I write this, I have a candle burning before an icon of the Virgin Mary that rests on the corner of my desk. I enter these words, I reach down inside and find them, I look up at the icon when I lose my focus.

I have also written entirely from within with no external focus, the cell within being its own center and centering. I suppose most of us move in and out this way, finding our center sometimes within, sometimes without. Just this morning I was reading about a figure skater who said that her young son centers her. And somewhere else I read about a monk who finds his center every day inside, where God dwells. I'm sure the figure skater finds her center inside, too, the center from which she skates, and the monk is centered at times by something outside.

The centering may be a ritual one performs. I have a yearly ritual that takes me away from the snow and cold. A ritual I started after my mother died: bringing up the amaryllis bulbs. I have two, Apple Blossoms, dazzling white with pale pink accents on the blossoms. The bulbs were planted in their terra-cotta pots several years ago. Now I seasonally bring them in after the first frost, cut off their green stems, bag them and place them in the cellar—dark and cool—till Christmas time. They remind me of birth because, though brought upstairs looking small and unattractive, I know there lies a hidden beauty inside that will burgeon and blossom and center me.

This small centering ritual is like the dynamic of entering into prayer: (1) I realize it's time to bring up the amaryllis bulbs again. (2) I open the cellar door and descend to the lowest level of the house. (3) The temperature changes—there's a rush of coolness as I walk down the steps. (4) I rummage about for the paper bags—where are they? Is everything inside okay again this year? (5) There's a damp, musty feel in the air, as of somewhere that's not been visited in a while, not been aired. (6) I bring the two bags up the stairs into the world where I live most of the time. (7) I place them in my window garden. (8) I wait for them to reveal their hidden mystery. I wait and water them once a week, and that becomes my centering prayer.

Scissors, Glue and Wrapping Paper

I am having lunch with a friend in Chicago just before Christmas. Chicago is one of my favorite cities any time of the year, but at Christmas time, like most cities, it puts on its finest—music and lights and friendlier faces, holiday sweaters and caps and coats transforming even the dour faces of the determined, compulsive shoppers.

My friend and I have not seen one another for a year. We are filling each other in on how it's been. She and her husband are both artists who work other jobs to pay the bills, work and pray for grants to help them continue their art in their free time. She is a receptionist/secretary to a team of psychologists and asks in the course of our conversation how she might design something new for one of the bi-yearly weekend retreats these therapists make together. We brainstorm awhile and finally hit on an idea that seems workable.

The word that keeps coming to me as she talks and as I reflect on many of the therapists I know—their seriousness, their harried countenances—is "play." Their retreat should not be a "head trip" or a "heart trip." They've enough of that every day. Therapists need to play, if they can.

We decide the retreat should be about making, doing—not thinking or emoting. So I suggest she gather the outdated magazines from the waiting room and have the therapists bring only scissors, glue and a large sheet of wrapping paper to their retreat. They will spend the weekend cutting out pictures or text that strikes them and assemble a collage of images and words. No theme, no purpose, other than play. The map that will emerge—if they do let go and play—will be the result of moving to a place within them that they've not visited for a long time, a place they visited often as children.

This simple activity will, I'm sure, be as important to this team of doctors as sitting at the feet of a guru or spiritual director. And in time, if it is repeated occasionally, it will lead them to the place inside where God dwells beyond thinking and feeling and willing, the place of perfect play where all is release and peace and unselfconsciousness.

What I have written here, I don't intend as a how-to exercise, but as a prompt for your own imagination to come up with something playful that will help you move to an area of your interior geography that you've abandoned or forgotten about or never even visited.

In addition, I record this Christmas time reunion to illustrate how a simple, shared meal can move into interiority and creativity. Our conversation moves to reflecting on play in our art—her photography, my poetry—and how in the arena within the camera's frame, the stanza (an Italian word for "room") of the poem's parameters, we both play, do things that the rules of our art enables us to do. Like the walls of a child's sandbox, the rules of one's art provide boundaries for a free play that we cannot perform outside those circumscribed boundaries. Prayer's parameters and rules do the same for us. They give us permission to let go of the often cynical inhibitions we've let surround the spiritual. We enter prayer as a sandbox where we can let go of the adult world's constrictive conventions and prejudices against turning (as Jesus counsels) and becoming a child again.

Within the sandbox of prayer I can cry and laugh and wail and praise. I can doubt and be afraid. I can simply sit and aimlessly throw sand into the air. It is safe there. And the rules facilitate, rather than inhibit, this kind of play—rules like the solitude of one's inner sandbox, temporary withdrawal from the world outside the sandbox, willingness to play, to set aside results, product, self-improvement.

What I'm talking about here is both a kind of doing and an attitude. If we take the spiritual life too seriously and make every prayer a life-or-death endeavor, then our expectations get in the way of the movement of the Other, of the Divine. One image of prayer I find most congenial is that of Adam and Eve walking with God in the Garden of Eden. Just walking, just taking in the Garden. No "What do we do now?" No "Where are we going? How long is this going to take? What are we doing this for?" Just walking in the garden of prayer for as long as it lasts. You may or may not sense God walking with you, but the garden itself will bring you peace, will bring you back, till one day you will understand God's been walking with you all along; that's why you came back. That's what really drew you to return to your garden walk. All creation, including God's, includes play and contains spaces where we can walk in the cool of the evening uninhibited and unafraid on paths opening on wonder and surprise.

Now, I've written all this, not in Chicago, but on a crippled Amtrak train sitting on a siding somewhere in Kansas. We've been without power for over two hours. It's now 9:00 A.M.; it's cold, the bathrooms are inoperable, the diner and club car are closed, there's an eerie silence on the train that I hadn't noticed till I started to write these sentences. I've been lost in the play of words on the page.

When I woke up to the dark, cold car, I could have fretted and become angry and complained—as I have in the past. But to what end? I chose instead to put into practice what I've been preaching in these pages and let this unanticipated inconvenience become a time of meditation.

Now it's 9:15 and we're beginning to move, slowly, almost imperceptibly. Slow may mean that all is not well yet; but it doesn't matter. We will arrive when we arrive. I try to make the interval peaceful and playful—play being something I recognize I need as much as the therapists I wrote about above. The feeling of helplessness to get the train moving fast is replaced by immersing myself in the present moment, which in turn becomes a graced time of playing in the garden of words.

Lectio Divina

Reading the psalms or any sacred text is a different reading from scanning *The New York Times* or *Christian Science Monitor*. This reading is like prayer. It is slow going. It keeps trying to become audible. We want to begin reading aloud, to chant the psalm, to murmur the text.

This manner of reading medievals called *lectio divina*, "divine reading" or "sacred reading." It called for a certain holy leisure and what they deemed a "vacancy" for God, an emptying and letting go of all worries and preoccupations in order to leave a space within for God to occupy. And the more one let go of, the larger the vacancy within that God would fill. Letting go, emptying the mind and heart of whatever was cluttering one's life, happened simultaneously with slowly, prayerfully reading the sacred text as if ingesting it, eating it. And as the words filled the soul, what was inconsequential clutter was pushed out; and the holy words became the simultaneously empty and full space where God dwells. Vacancy was not vacuum, therefore, but holy words that were somehow vehicle and container for the divine.

This is a long way from reading the morning paper with coffee and Danish in hand. This is reading as prayer; this is a divine activity, which Saint Augustine called leisure:

> Shortly after his baptism in 387 he went to Africa, feeling God's calling to practice *otium* ("leisure"), and founded a small community in the town of Thagaste. He declares the purpose of the group's common life is "to be deified by leisure." He strongly urges his dear friends to "love leisure, that you might refrain from all earthly pleasure, but remember that there is no place free from snares." He says elsewhere, "My leisure is not spent in nurturing idleness, but in exploring wisdom. . . . I draw back from distracting activities, and my spirit devotes itself to heavenly desires."[1]

This leisure, like that of the medieval monks, was a place and space which one took along throughout the day. Wherever one went, some phrase, some word from the reading rose to the conscious mind. Sometimes one would murmur the phrase, repeat the word aloud whenever it came to mind. The word found its way into the simplest or most mundane of tasks—milking the cows, ploughing the fields. "The Lord is my Shepherd," for example, or simply, "Shepherd," repeated over and over because that aspect of God's identity struck a chord and needed remembering, uttering aloud.

And thus goes a day when begun with *lectio divina*. The stimulation is from within, from a vacancy that is anything but vacant. The modern philosopher, Ivan Illich, writes:

> Both for the classical rhetor or sophist and for the monk, reading engages the whole body. However, for the monk, reading is not one activity but a way of life. Reading goes on whatever the monk does following his particular rule. This rule was established by St. Benedict and divides the day into two activities that are deemed equally important: *ora et labora*, pray and toil. Seven times a day the members of the small community of the ideal monastery meet in church. They listen to recitations done on one tone (*recto tono*), with rigidly defined inflections to mark questions, direct speech, or the end of a pericope, and they sing from the book of Psalms. In between, when the monk milks or plows, makes butter or chisels, the recitation in common turns into a subdued drone in which each picks his own lines. These lines are the road of his pilgrimage toward heaven, both when he prays and when he works. Reading impregnates his days and nights. This commitment to uninterrupted reading is of Jewish, rabbinical origin, like the plainchant which anchors the lines of the heart.[2]

This is the kind of reading one learns in prayer. And one keeps returning to prayer to re-learn and remember the importance of carrying over *lectio divina* into one's daily life. For we too soon forget to make a "vacancy" for God in a world of radio and TV,

newspapers and paperbacks, airplanes and subways and light-
ning-quick computers. Divine reading, like prayer, demands
leisure which, like peace, "comes dropping slow, / Dropping from
the veils of the morning to where the cricket sings." William
Butler Yeats's "The Lake Isle of Innisfree" is a veritable invitation and advertisement for prayer, not just for the monk but for
everyone for whom the stress and overstimulation of daily life
become too much to bear.

> I will arise and go now, and go to Innisfree,
> And a small cabin build there, of clay and wattles
>   made:
> Nine bean-rows will I have there, a hive for the
>   honeybee,
> And live alone in the bee-loud glade.
> And I shall have some peace there, for peace comes
>   dropping slow,
> Dropping from the veils of the morning to where the
>   cricket sings;
> There midnight's all a glimmer, and noon a purple
>   glow,
> And evening full of the linnet's wings.
> I will arise and go now, for always night and day
> I hear lake water lapping with low sounds by the
>   shore;
> While I stand on the roadway, or on the pavements
>   gray,
> I hear it in the deep heart's core.[3]

NOTES

[1] Ivan Illich, *In the Vineyard of the Text: A Commentary to Hugh's "Didascalicon"*
(Chicago and London: The University of Chicago Press, 1993), p. 62.
[2] Ibid., pp. 58–59.
[3] William Butler Yeats, "The Lake Isle of Innisfree," *Selected Poems of William
Butler Yeats* (New York: The MacMillan Company, 1962), pp. 12–13.

Praying with Icons

The word icon refers to a specific religious object. The icon I am most familiar with, the Russian icon, is made following an ancient ritual accompanied by prayer, fasting and silence. The palms of the iconographer are anointed with holy oil and prayers are chanted before each period of "writing" the icon. The very term, "writing," instead of "painting," differentiates this activity from what we usually think of when we envision the making of a painting. The reason for this is that an icon is more than a painting; it is a sacred object as well, that is anointed with oil upon completion and blessed by the priest before it is enthroned in sanctuary or home.

At an icon retreat I was privileged to observe, the master iconographer, Vladislav Andreyev, spoke repeatedly of "uncreated light," of contemplation, of *shekinah* (the uncreated presence of God in an icon), of praying with the icon you were writing. He began each writing session with the chanting of prayers, and he said the following prayer before he anointed the palms of the icon writer with holy balm:

> O You who so admirably imprinted Your features on the cloth sent to King Abgar of Edessa, and have so wonderfully inspired Luke, Your Evangelist and Apostle: Enlighten my soul and that of your servant: guide his/her hand that he/she may reproduce Your features, those of the Holy Virgin and Mother of God and all Your Saints, for the glory and peace of Your Holy Church. Spare him/her from temptations and diabolical imaginations in the name of Your Holy Mother, Saint Luke, and all the Saints.

The mention of the apostle Luke in this prayer derives from an ancient tradition that Saint Luke painted the first icon, an image of the Virgin and Child, blessed by the Virgin Mary herself and carried by Luke on his travels with Saint Paul.

All icons are painted according to prescriptions that resemble those for liturgical rites. One of the earliest books of such rules was *The Painter's Book of Mount Athos*. It gave instructions on how panels were to be prepared, for example, and the colors put on, and such details as the shapes of eyes and beards. The painters, too, according to the Hundred Chapters Ecclesiastical Council, convened by Tsar Ivan the Terrible in 1551, were to be "humble and mild . . . not given to vain words." They were to "live piously, not indulge in quarrels or drink, keep their souls pure, and live under the supervision of their spiritual guides."[1] At the workshop I attended, Divine Rules for the Icon Painter were recommended to each iconographer:

1. Before starting work, make the Sign of the Cross; pray in silence and pardon your enemies.
2. Work with care on every detail of your icon, as if you were working in front of the Lord himself.
3. During work, pray in order to strengthen yourself physically and spiritually; avoid all useless words and keep silence.
4. Pray in particular to the saint whose face you are painting. Keep your mind from distractions, and the saint will be close to you.
5. When you choose a color, stretch out your hands interiorly to the Lord and ask his counsel.
6. Do not be jealous of your neighbor's work; his/her success is your success, too.
7. When your icon is finished, thank God that his mercy granted you the grace to paint the holy images.
8. Have your icon blessed by putting it on the holy table of your parish church. Be the first to pray before it, before giving it to others.
9. Never forget:
   - the joy of spreading icons throughout the world,
   - the joy of the work of icon writing,
   - the joy of giving the saint the possibility to shine through his/her icon,
   - the joy of being in union with the saint whose face you are revealing.

Sister Jeannette Serra, s.s.c., herself an iconographer, has conducted retreats in which the participants are taught to pray with icons. She says of an icon's special religious significance:

> An icon is usually done on wood because wood comes from the tree of life. Wood also represents the cross of the Lord, our source of life. The icon is not meant to be a personal creation but rather a description of what one has contemplated. The icon comes from one's soul's center. One's concern is to proclaim the Word, to give glory to the Lord through the art.[2]

Sister Jeanette recommends that you

> pray with the icon that moves you—the one you find yourself drawn to, attracted by. Then, get to study the icon by knowing its history. This is like reading the Scriptures before you enter meditation.
>
> For your time of prayer, create your sacred space. Place the icon before you at eye level so you can look into the eyes. You may want to have a lighted candle before the icon as a symbol of the living Divine Presence.
>
> Begin with a prayer that expresses your desire to touch God's presence through the icon, to empty yourself for God to enter your sacred space. Allow yourself to enter into the prayer of gazing: Simply looking with love; simply looking with emptiness; simply looking with stillness—allowing yourself to be known by God through the icon's eyes.[3]

The icon I have been most drawn to from the time of my adolescence is the icon referred to in the West as "Our Lady of Perpetual Help," and in the Eastern Church as "Our Lady of the Passion."

The image of Our Lady of Perpetual Help draws me because of its association with my own mother, herself a perpetual help to me through the years, strong, uncomplaining, not holding on, but letting me hold on to her as does Mary in the icon of Our Lady of Perpetual Help. My mother's was the silence of the icon itself and that outward glance beyond me to those who may be "pursuing" me. Hers was the same look of inevitability, as if she knew, even when I was a child on her lap, the way things would turn out in the end, that reversal, slow or sudden, that signals an end preordained, sad, yet itself a further reversal that signals birth in death.

I think of my mother a lot in prayer, not just because she is now in heaven, but because of that look I see in Mary's icon and remember seeing in my mother's eyes. A prescience of death as inevitable, yet life-giving in the end. And because death is associated with that look of Mary and my mother and their cradling the child in their arms, death itself seems less terrifying, seems a return to the lap that cradled God and me, the boy-man who gazes upon the icon of Mary.

Convoluted as this may sound, it really is not, for mother, remembered, is an icon of Mary, and Mary is an icon of my own mother. I bring my mother with me into prayer when I bring Mary's icon with me.

Most of us bring some sort of icon to prayer, whether it be a real icon or an amulet, a picture, a sacred book, a memory, an expectation, a mental image. That "icon" gives focus to what we see in prayer, how we hear. Perhaps your icon is a constellation of images or objects. Catherine de Hueck Doherty has written of Russian Christians who set aside a room in their house or who have a cabin in the woods for prayer and meditation. It is called a *poustinia*, the Russian word for "desert" or "wilderness." From time to time they go there for twenty-four hours, taking only their "icons" of Bible, bread, water and a simple straw mattress for sleeping.

Once you have begun to make prayer a pattern in your life, certain portable objects or images emerge as icons of your way into more intense prayer. What they are reflects your own individuality and your own experience of what God uses to speak to your deepest center. You feel like anointing your hands before touching them, anointing your heart before reaching out to them in prayer, anointing your mind's eye for holding a remembered or imagined image. And like the iconographer, you reach for prayers that lead you into the mystery of God's presence made more tangible through these "icons" of your own life-in-God.

NOTES

[1] Arthur Voyce, *The Art and Architecture of Medieval Russia* (Norman, Okla.: University of Oklahoma Press, 1967), pp. 224–225.
[2] *Common Life,* The Edmundite Center, Burlington, Vt., Fall 1991, p. 16.
[3] Ibid., p. 17.

Prayer Walk

There's a knock on the door. Breakfast—I've retreated to a monastery to write and pray—and my first reaction is impatience. I've been distracted from my prayer and writing.

One of the first temptations of prayer is temporary excess. To plunge headlong into soul and forget the body. To tend wholly to the inner and neglect the outer. But as Saint Teresa of Avila used to caution her sisters, prayer is entering in, staying in a while and knowing when to come out again. My breakfast calls and I surrender the pen to its rest, the words to their quiet continuing presence without my probing and shaping.

I sit down to a small cheese and Canadian bacon omelette, orange juice, cubed cantaloupe, honey scones and homemade strawberry jam. I try not to think of what I've just written. I savor reverently what is before me. I tend to my body and thereby my soul, as well. For we are one, a wholeness, not fragmented, dichotomized into soul/body, outer/inner.

I look out the window at a robin resting on an autumn oak branch. I decide to take a walk after breakfast and notice as soon as I walk down the steps a child's red plastic cup on the sidewalk, a flowered, upholstered chair on a porch, a large elephant ear plant, a street clock I try to see not for the time it indicates but for its antique beauty.

All along the walk, like something sinister in my peripheral vision, my worries, troubles, fears, in short, "the world" I'll have to return to soon, keeps trying to block my vision. But I push these things away, not violently, not actually by pushing them down or away, but by attending to my walk, to what I see and hear. I surrender to this present moment's quiet and mystery. I stop thinking about what's not here before me.

Eventually my walk brings me back to this writing pad and I am reminded again of leaving and returning, the reality that kept trying to press in on me as I walked: "This is all fine, but you're going to have to go back and face the real world and nothing will be changed, or if it has, it will be for the worse, because you were not there being vigilant, watching over." Well, nothing's changed that I notice, but maybe I am, a bit.

My walk has quieted me, forced me to surrender work to leisure, given me practice in setting aside *doing* in order to let myself *be* with just strolling around the block. I say "strolling" because power-walking or jogging would be for me the substitution of one form of work for another, speed and accomplishment high on my expectation meter. When I stroll, there are not expectations, no *time* in which to "get it done." I let the stroll itself bring me home, which it does and I write down these words, which I wouldn't have had I not tended to something that was not particularly cerebral, had I not reverenced the simple but profound acts of eating and taking a stroll. Which brings me more naturally now to something I'd wanted to write about anyway:

Some people find it difficult to go into solitude for a week or so because they fear leaving, separation. What will happen to their loved ones if they are out of contact with them for a while? Wouldn't a weekend be safer than a whole week during which something terrible could happen? Maybe they should all go together into solitude?

This kind of anxiety, understandable as it is, is in itself a good reason for overcoming fear and risking solitude and separation as a journey into faith, trust.

We cannot live others' lives for them, nor can we watch over them always like a guardian angel. But we can tend, from time to time, to our own deep needs, our desire to commune more deeply with God, with our soul and thereby more deeply with those we love and worry about. But in order to do that communing, we have to leave loved ones at the door of our solitary retreat, so to speak, and not only loved ones, but anyone or anything we're preoccupied with. Like one who goes on pilgrimage, the prayer must consign to God's good care those left behind for a time.

And so, leaving our worries, tasks and loved ones in God's hands, we join all those who have made this journey before us. We enter the holy canyon and forest alone, yet in the company of hidden angels and prophets we meet in the deep heart's core and all around us. We begin the discovery of our own inner and outer landscape.

At Merton's Hermitage

Thomas Merton resigned his post as Master of Novices at the Monastery of Gethsemani in mid-August of 1965 and entered upon a more solitary life, living in a small, cinder block hermitage in a wooded area overlooking the old abbey in Nelson County, Kentucky.

—Brother Patrick Hart[1]

⟨❧⟩

Day One

That I should be here in Merton's hermitage! Sunday, March 19, 1995, the Feast of Saint Joseph. I am here, by exception and with special permission of Father Abbot, for a six-day private retreat—I, who when I read *The Seven Storey Mountain* as a boy of thirteen, thought I'd entered a world like that of the Arabian Nights, so fantastical did the story seem, so remote was Gethsemani, Kentucky, from New Mexico. And now forty-four years later, I sit at Merton's table, the one designed by Victor Hammer. At my back is the fireplace before which, still and empty, waits the rocker Jacques Maritain sat in when he visited Merton here.

The dwelling is quite spare. The smell of burnt wood permeates the hermitage, and I wonder how long before my clothes reek of smoke. The sunlight frets the concrete floor as it passes through the partially opened Venetian blinds. Firewood is stacked next to the fireplace. In the corner are several walking sticks.

On the table rest a few books I've pulled off the shelf from the original collection Merton had there when he left for the Far East in 1968: *The Portable Thoreau, The Mirror of Simple Souls* by an unknown French mystic of the thirteenth century, *Early Fathers from the Philokalia, Western Mysticism, The Mediaeval Mystics of England, The Flight from God* by Max Picard, *The*

Ancrene Riwle, The Book of the Poor in Spirit by a friend of God (fourteenth century), *A Guide to Rhineland Mysticism, A Treasury of Russian Spirituality, The Teaching of SS. Augustine, Gregory, and Bernard.*

How different from my three books on the same table. *The Bostonians* by Henry James, *Selected Poetry of Yehuda Amichai* and *Rainer Maria Rilke: New Poems 1907.*

I walk out on Merton's porch and am overwhelmed with stars, the whole sky alive with their lights as when a boy I would look up into the New Mexico sky in wonder.

Stars and daffodils and a dead bluebird. When I cleaned the ashes out of the wood stove earlier in the afternoon, there on the grate, not fallen through like the ashes, was a dead bluebird, its tiny feet aloft and rigid, as if clinging upside down to a branch no longer there. I lifted the bird reverently from the cold grate and buried him on the path behind the hermitage. I placed two twigs in the sign of the cross on the earth beneath which his blue feathers would now begin to fade into the black Kentucky soil. Would I have noticed a dead bird as I rushed to class from our friary on Pleasant Street in inner-city Cincinnati?

Maybe this is the beginning of contemplation, the part about the bird, I mean. At least it strikes me that finding the bird and burying it was the beginning of *Franciscan* contemplation, not because of Saint Francis and the birdbath thing, but because of Saint Francis' reverence for all things, his sacramental eyes that saw the Incarnation concretely in the sacredness of everything animate and inanimate. "Be praised, My Lord," he sang, "through all that You have made."

When I was out earlier, the sky full of stars, I looked for but did not find the moon. Now getting ready to retire, I look up and there is the moon, yellow, just beginning to wane, low on the horizon to the left of the hermitage's front window. The silent moon. I go out on the porch for a better view. Silent the moon in rising, silent in its sentinel watching.

I retire to the bedroom, where a single bed is pushed up close against the wall, but return to the front room again, just to check the moon. When was the last time I did anything like that? My hermitage retreat must be beginning.

I care now about the moon, when before I came here all my care was on what to bring. I remembered Thoreau's "simplify, simplify, simplify." But just in case, I brought two loaves of bread, canned soups, fruit, laptop computer, underclothes, socks, sweat pants, extra jeans, extra shoes, umbrella, three coats (one for cold, one for cool, one for rain), flashlight, cellular phone (notice how I sneaked in computer and cellular phone the way adultery is sneaked into confession between harmless peccadilloes), batteries, two tape recorders (one that plays only, one that also records), books and books and books, juices and candy, two cameras (one in fact did jam and I had to use the other), binoculars, Sorel boots (in case of a surprise snowstorm the first week of spring), pills and pills and Skin-So-Soft (in case of early mosquitoes), whiskey (Heaven Hill bourbon, Merton's favorite)—in case of snake bite or for hot toddies should I catch a chill.

All of that and more, and now all I see is the moon, all I care about is the silence and the night full of stars.

⟨⟐⟩

Day Two

I had thought the silence might frighten me. Instead it's more than comfortable here—I'm happy. Especially with the sun rising now where the moon surprised me last night.

And no phone ringing. I've unplugged the cellular phone, put it away.

I'm lounging with a cup of coffee, having slept well. I'm following the Italian dictum, *dolce far niente*, "sweetly doing nothing," as I prepare for morning Mass in Merton's chapel. There's a small ceramic cross here, fashioned for Merton by Ernesto Cardenal, the Nicaraguan priest and poet, who was for a time in the late fifties Merton's novice at Gethsemani Abbey. There are three icons as well. None is the original icon given to Merton by Marco Pallis in 1965. That marvelous Greek, probably Macedonian, icon from around 1700 is now wisely preserved in the archives of the abbey.

Merton describes the icon thus: "The Holy Mother and Child and then on panels that open out, St. Nicholas and St. George, St. Demetrius and St. Chorlandros—whoever that is."[2]

Merton wrote to Pallis that he never tired

> of gazing at it. There is a spiritual presence and reality about it, a true "Thaboric" light, which seems unaccountably to proceed from the Heart of the Virgin and Child as if they had One heart, and which goes out to the whole universe. It is unutterably splendid. And silent. It imposes a silence on the whole hermitage. . . .[3]

Earlier I took a walk down the road to where I could see the abbey unobstructed by trees and brush. Photographed the back of the chapel and monastery. Back here in the hermitage, I take in the silence Merton's icon bequeathed to this cinder-block dwelling. I recall the distinctions of silence that John F. Teahan made in his *Cistercian Studies* paper about the place of silence in Merton's life. He divides silence into public, ascetical and meditational.

> The public or ritual use of silence . . . facilitates solemnity, reverence, recollection, and sense of mystery. . . . [Ascetical silence], the attempt to rescue physical quiet from verbal overload, is normally considered a means to the more important goal of calming interior consciousness, an important prerequisite for many forms of mystical experience. . . . A final type of religious silence is associated with the practice of meditation. . . . The silence of meditation directs attention away from everyday . . . turbulence, fosters inner calm and thus makes the meditator more aware of innermost self. . . ."[4]

The purpose of religious solitude is to be alone with God, to find myself in God, and in God to see and understand my communion with everything that is. In solitude and silence I come to know the interconnection of all things. In their aloneness in God, who is their source, all things are both unique and in union. To know the One in my own aloneness is to know the many. Even the word "alone" contains the word "one" and a suggestion of the word "all."

I enter into solitude and silence in order to know that I am not alone. In aloneness I experience that all are one and one is somehow all.

Franciscan eremitism follows through on the implications of such a discovery of the many in the one. I enter into solitude to rediscover my connectedness with all that is; I leave the hermitage for the open road impelled by charity to make manifest in my life and relationship with others that we are all in God. That relationship ultimately comes down to seeing, listening and responding in charity.

But service, doing, even seeing and listening dulls, and I enter solitude again in order to find again my sight and hearing, to rediscover the One who is the source of my reason for listening to and serving the many.

In silence and solitude I relearn that I am in others and they are in me, whether or not we are physically present to one another. My own uniqueness discovered in the One who made me and dwells in me, is my simultaneous discovery of everything that is in the same One who inhabits silence and solitude—a silence and solitude I carry with me in the tabernacle of my deepest self. A silence and solitude I forget is there when I abandon retreating into that center and allow myself to be distracted by the proliferation of things and people, by noise and sound that obscure the way back into the center of myself where I realize how deeply connected I am to others. If I continue to immerse myself in other things and people, I paradoxically become alienated from them and myself. I lose myself in them and resent their demands on my time and attention. If I take the time to withdraw periodically into silence and solitude, I reconnect to myself and others from whom I've grown alienated.

Silence, solitude and communion are all complementary. In communion I know solitude; in solitude I know communion; in silence I know both solitude and communion. For God's silence is God's speaking beyond words and ideas. It is God's communication to the heart silent and alone, listening beyond words for the truth of its oneness and communion.

All of which sounds terribly abstract. I had better go out and look at the daffodils.

 srys

Day Three

I'm back from yesterday's daffodils. Seeing them and loving them made me realize that when I came here to Merton's hermitage, I was angry about a lot of things: like politics and politicians, the incessant chatter of news people whose talk is largely half-truths and sometimes downright lies—for effect or ratings, or whatever else words become when they are detached from truth and reflection.

I was appalled at the sensationalism of talk shows and of the coverage of the O. J. Simpson trial. The invasion of privacy, the lack of taste and decorum and basic human decency depressed me. What was happening to the world? How could we permit the atrocities in Bosnia to go unnoticed, except in passing, and spend hours and hours and hours on the O. J. Simpson trial?

And now here in solitude, I'm no longer angry or alienated from those "others" who don't think or act like me. I feel, rather, compassion and love and connectedness, communion with all of them. I see myself in those I criticized; they are in me and I in them. They, too, long for solitude and silence where they can find themselves again. They, like me, are really solitudes trying to connect with one another. We all feel disconnected when we fail or refuse to be alone long enough to know we are not alone.

All great religious leaders entered into solitude and there heard the word of God. When they returned again to community with others, they shared God's word. Those who heard and became disciples of that word, if they, too, did not enter into solitude with the word they had heard from their teacher or prophet, often used the word they'd heard to make other words that divide and separate. These other words breed hatred and even war among other hearers of these new words that have nothing of solitude and silence in them and therefore do not derive from God but from the perversity of the human heart when it refuses the silence wherein God speaks to it.

So in a very real way we enter into silence in order to keep from killing each other. We find in solitude the reason why we need to love one another or lose our very selves.

Already on my second night at the hermitage I wished I'd brought a small TV to relax with late at night. But I had not brought one, and so I was forced to look elsewhere. That's when I began to really see the hermitage, the woods, the tone of the evening. A thunderstorm was gathering and I went out onto the porch to watch the black clouds gather. Lightning began to crack around the hermitage and I withdrew to the safety of the living room where I already had a fire roaring in the wood stove. I wanted to stand by the large window next to the stove, but the trees were beginning to bend in the strong wind, and I was afraid here on this knoll one of the trees would be hit by lightning, especially the tall beech next to the window.

I retreated to the kitchen and then into the chapel where I could watch the incredible electrical display moving east, where I'd seen the moon the night before and the sun rising that same morning. The thunder and lightning lasted only about twenty minutes, about the length of a half-hour sitcom minus the commercials.

I went back to the kitchen, and light was breaking in the west even as the last flashes of lightning strobed the interior of the hermitage. Light following light. As the storm approached, there were patches of light in the sky over the hermitage and the western horizon was black and thunderous. Now the east was black as light broke in the west, the sun's last rays illumining a sliver of horizon where the black clouds were lifting, moving east with the rest of the storm.

The whole thing was better than most half-hour TV shows and I felt much more involved with the consequences of what might happen before it was over.

Then, just as I thought it was all over, the grounds in front of the hermitage lit up like a visitation of angels, and the town of New Hope, far in the distance beyond, shone like a painting of Bethlehem's first Christmas with its flood of light from the Magi's guiding star.

I usually don't carry on like this about TV shows, nor do I write about what I've watched on the screen. But here in the hermitage I was seeing something actually happening, not seeing what the camera's eye is seeing, whether or not it's live or recorded, fact or fiction. I was directing my own eyes east and west, before and after, not watching what someone else has decided I should see.

How often I've been shocked or felt pity for victims of the camera's merciless, invasive eye. Compassion, mercy or simply decency would have moved me to look aside, allow the person or scene its private sorrow or shame or pain. How cruel is the camera's eye, or more accurately, those who direct and aim and focus that indifferent lens.

This knowledge, too, I will take home with me. I've seen, reflected, written and been led into prayer that centers on the incarnate, not the televised, event—a storm over the hermitage, light flaring over the town of New Hope.

When darkness falls at the hermitage, I am at first apprehensive, even fearful. Night. Within and without we feel more vulnerable, especially in a strange place, removed from the security of friends and loved ones. We notice every small sound until we can identify it and dismiss it. We wonder what ghosts might inhabit such places deep in the woods where there are no streetlights, no passing cars, no sirens and horns. Or are the ghosts only our own fears?

I take up a book to distract me, I do chores like stoke the stove, wash dishes, order the table where I will write in the morning. I pray Divine Office in the chapel before the Blessed Sacrament. My fears dissipate.

Routine, familiar and not so familiar, begins to fill the night hours. I pen some notes, pray, take up the novel I brought with me, *The Bostonians*. I put it down, wish I'd brought something lighter, surrender to silence, solitude, oncoming drowsiness.

☙❧

Day Four

Already on the fourth day in the hermitage I begin to understand the importance of domestic chores. I wake and put on the coffee water, open the blinds and welcome the morning. Shaking down the ashes from the grate into the ash pan at the bottom of the stove, and carrying in wood and sweeping the floor afterwards and lighting the newspapers under the kindling wood, all of these mundane, small activities become the vehicles of grace for me. I putter about the hermitage, make the bed, wash the breakfast dishes, sweep the porch; and something begins to order itself inside me as I order my external world. The ordering and puttering become a kind of prayer, a way of attending to the human, which is a way of attending to the divine, charged as we are and the world is with the presence of God.

Domestic chores also become simply something to do. One cannot pray and meditate unendingly. There is a rhythm to life lived anywhere that calms the heart if we surrender to the necessities of the world around us and the world within. In a letter to the poet Clayton Eshleman, Merton writes of the simplicity of his own rhythm at the hermitage: "I get some writing done, read a fair amount, chop wood, think a lot."

Instead of being wrenched and tortured by the demands of others, the greed and competition, the frenetic pace of the modern world, if I can bring myself to retreat from time to time, if for no other reason than to listen to my own heart and body, then this other, simpler, often more domestic rhythm begins to modulate the heart's nervous pounding. Simple, deliberate acts humanize what has become, little by little, a robot-like existence. "'Tis a gift to be simple," as the old Shaker hymn has it.

The hope, of course, is that I take this new rhythm with me when I return to other responsibilities, that what I have experienced within, I can return to as to a funding memory of where I need to be, how I need to be if I am to be fully human with myself, fully loving toward others.

I know from past experience that what I learn here in the hermitage won't last long in the onslaught of the "real world." But I know also that the experience will beckon me to return, to enter into retreat again and again until it does, in fact, become portable like an inner habit I carry with me, though it may lie dormant in the face of other demands.

It's about discovering anew my true self, which I find, paradoxically, when I forget myself in simple tasks: in an ordering routine, silence, solitude and, above all, in God. For every quiet, ordering task, every murmured prayer, every contemplation of tree or flower or weather, is a losing of myself in the other in preparation for losing myself in *the* Other, God. God, who comes not when I am straining, twisting the divine arm to reveal its presence, but who comes when I least expect, when I'm sweeping the hermitage floor, lighting the fire, drinking a cup of coffee. God is gift. God comes when I am quiet, when I surrender to the rhythm of my own heart, when I take time to re-find the time that is not clock-time, chronological time, but inner time, fullness of time, the time of mystery.

I look at my watch and see the secondhand move, and I become anxious, I look at the morning sun and don't see it move, though I know it will continue to be in different places in the sky as the earth moves, and time becomes something other than linear movement.

Time is something I don't see but rest in as in God's presence which affects the tone and color of everything. Time reveals itself as God does in brief epiphanies that come as intuitions, glimpses of something I can't quite see but know is there affecting everything I do, everything I am.

Today is the first day of spring. The view from the hermitage is that of a clear, crisp morning after a night of lightning and thunder and wind clearing the sky for this grace of morning. Gratitude rises in me like the sun. I am suddenly immensely grateful for the silence and for simple things like naps and leisure and long walks in the woods and food, things I have not given sufficient thanks for before.

Here at the hermitage, for example, I look forward to the simple meals. Lots of fruit and homemade bread and strong, stinky, marvelous Trappist cheese that Brother Patrick gave me when I arrived. Someone baked me a loaf of pumpkin bread, too, which I brought along for a breakfast substitute for oatmeal a couple of mornings. And coffee for mornings, Earl Grey tea for late afternoons. And some M&M's I said I wouldn't bring but did and have enjoyed inordinately.

I feel thankful, too, for a new awareness of time, pregnant time that gives birth to one's own private revelation, one's own insight, only in the fullness of time, when gestation has come full term within and God is born from the soul. This gratitude and this new awareness of time is common to all traditions, to all who enter solitude in order to pray and listen to silence.

ɔ৵ɔ

Day Five

Each day here I ventured farther into the woods surrounding the hermitage, and each night I stayed out longer looking at the stars. At first I holed up in the hermitage as in a safe refuge from whatever was out there. I pretty much kept to the main fireplace and woodstove living room where there was light and warmth and a door I could secure. Like someone put down in the wilderness I needed a hut, a cabin, an anchoring place.

The same is true of the human soul. It stays indoors at first, only tentatively exploring the other, the unknown the seemingly unsafe. It fears the dark. What I see my body doing, exploring, is what my soul is doing as well.

On the fifth afternoon I leave the hermitage to travel to a small grocery mart in Culvertown, a couple of miles down the road. My emotions surprise me. It feels almost like a sin to leave, and I can't wait to return. This gift is so precious, so rare, I don't want to waste a minute of it—then I realize I am back in linear time again and surrender to what needs to be done and return to the hermitage after picking up a head of lettuce and a half pint of milk—and all is well again.

I guess I'm growing accustomed to this place. I wonder why, though? Is this just a romantic junket like a Caribbean cruise, something different, a fling in the woods pretending to be Thoreau or Merton or anyone else who's entered solitude without a car waiting to whisk them away as soon as possible after the quick fix in a hermitage? Well, I've done the hermitage thing; now what?

I don't think it's that at all. It's certainly not a cruise; no luxuries here, no fellow travelers. Why, then, am I here?

The only answer I can give is that somehow we gravitate to solitude and silence as to the ground of our being; but something has to happen inside for us to act upon that simple truth. What that is is as varied as are the human beings who find their way to a place of hermitage. It has something to do with wanting to find God or ourselves, which is the same thing. For only in God do we know who we are and only in our deepest selves do we find God. Our selves in solitude and prayer, or our selves loving selflessly another or others, or our selves responding to a sacred ritual.

In religious hermitage there are all of these: God, self, solitude, prayer, charity and ritual. But the key to all of them is prayer. For it is in prayer that God finds us and we find ourselves, find love, have the need to ritualize our experience.

Nor is God's finding us always an experience of sweetness and light. It may be like the divine wrestling Jacob experienced in the Book of Genesis of the Bible:

Jacob was left alone; and a man wrestled with him until daybreak. When the man saw that he did not prevail against Jacob, he struck him on the hip socket; and Jacob's hip was put out of joint as he wrestled with him. Then he said, "Let me go for the day is breaking." But Jacob said, "I will not let you go, unless you bless me." So he said to him, "What is your name?" And he said, "Jacob." Then the man said, "You shall no longer be called Jacob, but Israel, for you have striven with God and with humans, and have prevailed." Then Jacob asked him, "Please tell me your name." But he said, "Why is it that you ask my name?" And there he blessed him. So Jacob called the place Peniel, saying, "For I have seen God face to face, and yet my life is preserved." (Genesis 32:24–30)

Prayer is often a struggle, a wrestling with ourselves to quiet down, to focus, to listen. A wrestling with faith to believe we're not just talking to ourselves but are in fact in dialogue with a God we cannot hear. A wrestling with the God we do hear deep inside those insights and convictions that invite us to change, to begin moving out of our self-preoccupation into charity, other-centeredness motivated by God's love for us. A wrestling at last with a God who may not be who we thought God was, who may even wound us that we might know with whom we wrestle.

But no matter how prolonged the wrestling, in the end we know from the peace in our hearts that it is God we've been struggling with; it is God who finally has our attention.

This sort of dynamic happens in practically all prolonged, or even at times in short, prayer. We settle down, try to move to that quiet place within, try to become conscious of our breathing, its rhythm, its calming effect. We begin to feel we are being breathed by the Other we have come to listen to, to surrender to. And then, in spite of our focus, all our concerns and worries rush in. How are we going to pay the mortgage? Who's going to pick up the kids from the pool? What am I going to cook for supper? Did I remember to pay the light bill? Was I supposed to call Aunt Clara? Will I pass algebra? Will I get a job? Why doesn't he/she love me the way I love her/him? Do I have an ulcer? Will God cure Uncle Frank? And on and on.

We wrestle with these and myriad other concerns, trying to put them out of our minds, trying to focus on the one thing necessary; and mostly we fail at it until the very end of the time we've set aside for prayer. If it's an hour, usually in the last ten minutes or so, we begin to settle down and in, and peace comes. Comes we don't know how, but we suspect it's from God, and the wound that the headache, worry and struggle have caused us is worth it, and we remember the place where we were wounded. We want to return there tomorrow for the five or ten minutes of mysterious peace. And we do because we got through the day better after the wrestling and its attendant peace.

Sometimes, as in Jacob's other experience of God, we want to ritualize our experience in some tangible way.

> He came to a certain place and stayed there for the night, because the sun had set. Taking one of the stones of the place, he put it under his head and lay down in that place. And he dreamed that there was a ladder set up on the earth, the top of it reaching to heaven; and the angels of God were ascending and descending on it. . . . Then Jacob woke from his sleep and said, "Surely the LORD is in this place—and I did not know it!" And he was afraid and said, "How awesome is this place! This is none other than the house of God, and this is the gate of heaven."

> So Jacob rose early in the morning, and he took the stone that he had put under his head and set it up for a pillar and poured oil on the top of it. . . . "[A]nd this stone, which I have set up for a pillar, shall be God's house; and of all that you give me I will surely give one-tenth to you." (Genesis 28:11–12, 16–18, 22)

Like Jacob we are moved to set up a pillar, a stone, or hollow out a place in the earth, a womb, a kiva, or we are moved to turn toward Mecca, to pray at Jerusalem's wailing wall, to go to a mosque or synagogue or church or meeting house, to go on pilgrimage to our own holy place, that place where God dropped a ladder down to us. Or we want to prolong the experience or allow time to let the experience of God in prayer take root, become a pillar of strength within us.

And so we enter into our inner hermitage where prayer becomes an intensification and celebration of these daily wrestlings with God, an act of profound thanksgiving and commemoration of the wound and the ladder we carry with us daily.

It is interesting that in the story of Jacob's ladder, which comes before the wrestling with God, God reveals "I am the LORD, the God of Abraham your father and the God of Isaac" (Genesis 28:13), but in the wrestling, God asks, "Why is it you ask my name?" (Genesis 32:29). God knows that Jacob knows, as we do, whom we are wrestling, even if we have no image or name for him.

The Tao Te Ching says:

> Names can be named, but not the Eternal Name.
> Its name is Formless.
> Listen to it, but you cannot hear it!
> Its name is Soundless.
> Grasp at it, but you cannot get it!
> Its name is *Incorporeal*.[5]

This, too, is what we find in prayer. For most of us, there is no tangible person to wrestle with; there is no voice of God; there is only Formless, Soundless, Incorporeal. But we know that, too, is God. God comes to us as God will, and we know when we have been in the presence of the Divine. We know it in the peace that follows upon the experience, even if the experience itself is a wrestling. We know it in the impulse to love more selflessly, to reach out to the poor, the despised, the rejected. We know it in that Formless, Soundless, Incorporeal Other we bear with us that transforms us little by little from superficial, outer-dominated persons, to persons who act from the inside out rather than feeling always acted upon, pushed and shoved and forced to go where we don't really want to go, to be who we know we aren't.

⟨∿⟩

Day Six

Leaving. When it comes time to leave this solitude, I begin to have the same feelings I had upon leaving home. I am anxious, a bit sad, wondering how it will be to "face" everything again. Will I be better able to handle things? Will I continue to feel as whole as I do now, as close to God? Will I be able to take something of this experience with me and hold it for a while?

And the birds, the daffodils, the woodstove, the other solitudes I have met here, what of them? Won't I need to return again to this place, this feeling, this quiet that I've found? I know I'll take it with me and that eventually it will seem all used up, and I'll need to return to refund the place in the heart that this experience has opened up.

Hermitage, like prayer, is for doing again and again. For what you find there and bring from it you seldom find elsewhere. It needn't be the same physical locale, but the same kind of experience whose geography you recognize each time you find it again.

And what about the return I'm so worried about? Won't it be like the hermitage itself, something I'll get used to? And won't I grieve, or at least miss, my time in solitude?

Thomas Merton spent his whole monastic life fretting in one way or another whether he should leave the cenobitic, communal, Trappist life for a more eremetical, solitary life. And even toward the end of his life, when he finally had his hermitage in the woods, he would return to the monastery to reconnect with his brothers. Merton's secretary, Brother Patrick Hart, remembers how at the beginning of his hermitage life, Merton, in blue jeans and with an empty water jug hung from his shoulder, would return to the monastery to give his conferences to the novices and young monks. At times he would open these conferences to the whole community, as when he talked on literary themes like the poetry of Rilke or the novels of Faulkner.[6]

But Merton was always happy to return to his hermitage. The short distance between Merton's hermitage and the abbey, which he could see from his front porch, and the tension between the two, is the distance and tension we experience upon entering and leaving a hermitage. We want to stay, but we need community, companionship, human love; we want community but we want some solitude, silence.

That tension brings us to the hermitage and allows us to leave. Like a pilgrimage to a holy shrine, there is always the return and the subsequent longing to go on pilgrimage again. Even Merton, who had in the end found the solitary hermitage he wanted all his life, left that hermitage to go on pilgrimage to the

East, where he learned what he must have known all along. The rimpoches (Buddhist "teachers") had all warned him against absolute solitude and stressed compassion. They advised being in solitude most of the year and then coming out for a while.

For most of us it is the other way around, and each experience of prayerful solitude makes it more so: being with others most of the year, but needing to enter solitude for a while, as well. That rhythm, that silent music of the soul.

NOTES

[1] Brother Patrick Hart, *The Literary Essays of Thomas Merton* (New York: New Directions, 1981), p. 497.
[2] John Howard Griffin, *Follow the Ecstasy* (Mansfield, Tex.: JHG Editions/Latitudes Press, 1983), p. 56.
[3] *The Hidden Ground of Love: The Letters of Thomas Merton on Religious Experience and Social Concerns,* p. 474.
[4] John F. Teahan, "The Place of Silence in Thomas Merton's Life and Thought," *Cistercian Studies,* Number 42, 1981, pp. 92–93.
[5] Thomas Merton, *A Thomas Merton Reader*, Thomas P. McDonnell, ed. (New York: Image Books, 1974), pp. 295–296.
[6] Cf. *The Literary Essays of Thomas Merton,* Brother Patrick Hart, ed. (New York: New Directions, 1981), p. 497.

PART FIVE:

Landscape and Soul

My Father

One of my earliest and most vivid childhood land-scapes is of my father fly-fishing. He's on Pine River outside Durango, Colorado, where we lived for a time in my childhood and where my father was born. His fly rod is poised over the trout-rich stream like a diviner's rod.

It seemed to me, even then, that he was doing more than drawing out trout. He was, in fact, as I learned years later, be-coming what gave him life: being a fisherman. Each time he threw his rod and reel into the trunk of the Chevy and lit out for a river or trout lake, my father was in effect going on retreat, his rod and reel the means by which he would enter that place within where he felt good about himself, felt at peace, felt that everything in his life came together whenever he stood in the middle of a trout stream arcing flies across the water's mouth.

The image of fly-fishing is archetypal. We've seen it in movies and books like *A River Runs Through It* and *Fly-Fishing Through the Mid-Life Crisis*. We've seen it in paintings of the solitary fisher standing serenely in a river named Solitude. That image is central to me because it derives from my own childhood, the great storehouse of images we continue to return to.

A few months after my father died, I decided to go on a fishing pilgrimage to honor his memory, to revisit the image of my Dad fly-fishing. These are some of the word passages I made on that pilgrimage:

I step into the cool, fast-running stream, and they pull me in, the memories of Dad, his creel hanging from his left shoulder, his left hand in constant motion easing the line in and out, his right hand waving the bamboo fly rod like a wand over streams in Colorado, New Mexico and Arizona. His wading boots droop their tops about his knees as he stands on the bank or they hug his hips out in the water where he walks for miles, stumbling at times, slipping on slick rocks, steadying himself as he stalks the elusive trout. His canvas hat is slouched down over his ears; it covers his bald head from the sun, shields his eyes from blinding rays striking the stream's surface. His pants, ever baggy, seemingly ready to fall down, ride his slim waist under his prominent belly. He's fly-fishing, and I'm photographing his slow movement downstream. It is two years before his death silences the swish of the fly rod I've listened to since I was a boy scarcely able to walk. Fly-fishing, the constant ritual he performed in good times and bad, in sickness and in health, week after week after week.

There was never a time Dad wasn't fly-fishing, except for the four years of the Pacific campaign during World War II, 1942 to 1946. He donned his fishing vest with the earnestness of a priest putting on a chasuble. He fished more than anyone I've ever known. And like the prayer-practice of a monk, fishing shaped and formed who he was. He retreated into fishing in every pain and trouble, on feast days and in Ordinary Time. He wanted to die in a trout stream in Colorado. And had he not died quietly in his sleep preparing for a morning fishing trip, he would have had a good chance of doing so, the way he kept stumbling through dangerous waters even at age eighty-one.

Now I hold his fly rod in my own inept hand unsure of its trajectory, the magic of its action. I'm wearing Dad's brown two-tone Red Ball waders and one of his old fly vests, once white, now faded almost to tan and patched with pieces of an old green and brown striped shirt. I'm casting his Browning Silaflex rod with the old Blue Marlin automatic reel he used so many times.

I fling the J. H. Special fly he designed outward in a gentle arcing motion, water dripping from line and fly like an aspergil's head blessing the water. I'm reaching back and out and in looking for my father. I work the fly, I try to seduce the browns running predictably, mechanically, as if they've been there beneath the surface jerking, holding steady under rocks, for as long as I've been looking down into water, their ritual motions as programmed as the gene codes written into our very selves by God. We dance our unique dance, touching, moving together in our separate elements, water and air sustaining us in a rhythm broken only when a trout breaks from the water's surface, the fly caught where I felt the lip's tug and jerked it firmly into the almost transparent skin, lifting the wriggling, slippery mottled brown carefully, keeping it in the water, where I unhook what can't be kept and drop it back into its own choreography as the fin splatters its dive deep into the stream's safety.

I've returned the trout to water because what can't be kept is the catching itself, the moment of meeting between human and fish, that recognition, that need to surrender the fish to its own element. What can be kept is the caught, and that is not what I'm here for. I'm trying to catch a memory of contact, a meeting with more than fish, that I have to keep returning to its own waters, keep coming back and fishing for; finding it, letting it go again until my own fishing replaces the fishing I'm trying to emulate.

I'm fishing, trying to bring back what can't be brought back: my Dad fishing. But with each fish caught and returned, danced with and seduced, I'm becoming what I so admired in Dad. I'm continuing the tradition, keeping the magic of fly rod and fly alive. I can't hold on to what I'm really fishing for except in the fishing for. The doing is the memory alive that is as evanescent and unkeepable as the moment of meeting between a trout and a human being. Only a dead trout is keepable; the trout alive surfaces and dives below the surface for as long as the fisherman continues the ritual of mantling rod and reel, slipping leader and fly onto line, and arcing the fly over the water's surface, knowing in the doing communion with more than fish and river water.

Fly-fishing reminds me that I can't hold in prayer what I can't hold in fishing. The caught and kept dies; the meeting, the encounter lives in the memory kept alive in the ritual that remembers the meeting's knowing.

Do this in memory of me, I hear him saying, the old fisherman with the slouched-down hat and the waders I'm now wearing. *Do this, and you will know me in doing what I did.*

The whole of the Christian's day-to-day life is based on that kind of remembering. We know the Lord in our walking his footsteps, taking up the cross with him, dying and rising in our following the way of him who went before us. "Therefore be imitators of God, as beloved children, and live in love, as Christ loved us and gave himself up for us, a fragrant offering and sacrifice to God" (Ephesians 5:1–1).

Identification with my father in fly-fishing. Identification with Christ in living the gospel. Both require practice, silence and seeing. In short, the art of prayer and of fly-fishing is craft plus contemplation. Craft becomes art through contemplation, as in this, one of my favorite passages from Hemingway's "Big, Two-Hearted River."

> The river was there. It swirled against the log piles of the bridge. Nick looked down into the clear, brown water, colored from the pebbly bottom, and watched the trout keeping themselves steady in the current with wavering fins. As he watched them they changed their positions by quick angles, only to hold steady in the fast water again. Nick watched them a long time.
>
> He watched them holding themselves with their noses into the current, many trout in deep, fast-moving water, slightly distorted as he watched far down through the glassy convex surface of the pool, its surface pushing and swelling smooth against the resistance of the log-driven piles of the bridge. At the bottom of the pool were the big trout. Nick did not see them at first. Then he saw them at the bottom of the pool, big trout looking to hold themselves on the gravel bottom in a varying mist of gravel and sand, raised in spurts by the current.[1]

The young Nick Adams we see in this passage will fish well, we know, because he sees well. He contemplates the trout, identifies with them, knows them in silence and solitude. Living well requires what fishing well requires, this kind of seeing, the silence, the solitude of contemplation that leads, over a lifetime, to seeing well enough to be at peace, even in the face of seeming defeat, like the old Cuban fisherman of Hemingway's *The Old Man and the Sea*. He is at peace even when the sharks destroy his great prize catch before he can bring it in to port. He blames no one but himself as he tows the mere skeleton of the fish behind his small boat. He asks himself what beat him, then says aloud, "Nothing. I went out too far."

⚜

I'm here on the river, an only child, trying to carry on the family tradition. It's as if the mantle of Dad's love for fishing has been placed on my shoulders, and I love its feel. I didn't when Dad was alive. At least I didn't know I could love fly-fishing. In my own mind it was something I wasn't supposed to like that much. It was what Dad did, and did better than anyone. I was the apprentice, the learner, the disciple.

How often that is the case. We remain our parents' children until they die, and then suddenly we're grown-ups. We take their place. We want to keep them alive, do well what they did well and wanted us to do well, but somehow kept disappointing them in when they were alive. And so we begin to remember how they did things: the recipes, the order of tools in the garage, where and how to get the best bargains, how the table looked at Thanksgiving, where and how the Christmas ornaments were stored, the trick of threading a needle or putting a fishing fly on a leader, how to clean fish, gut wild game, what seasonings you use to get the "wild" taste out of venison, how to keep books and records and how to prepare tax returns the way Dad did, order canning supplies where Mom did.

We ask brothers and sisters, uncles and aunts, if we can't remember. We keep reaching back in memory trying to keep alive and pass on and reverence what has been given us in trust and love.

It is this dynamic that informs much of one's interior prayer life over the years, only here it is trying to remember and recreate salvation history, what has been passed on to us by generations of those who have desired to know, love and serve God. They have told us in word and action what we in prayer are trying to remember, reverence, carry out in our own lives, then pass on to others.

As a Franciscan friar, I am much aware that there are two human fathers who have formed who I am: my Dad and my holy father Saint Francis. At times they work as opposites within me, one taking me fishing and hunting, the other leading me away from fishing and hunting and the consequent death of fish and animal. These are the two valences that struggle within me and that I am reminded of on this fishing retreat. I am trying to reconcile these opposites, trying in one sense to leave both "fathers" and become my own person.

We do that, all of us, when our father dies and we begin to see some "father" who has been vying with our earthly father for ascendancy within us. For me the other "father," Saint Francis, has had the greater part of my attention and allegiance from the time of my adolescence. His influence over me triggered and facilitated the break with my dad that every boy experiences in trying to find himself. In the process there were other "fathers," Franciscan priests and brothers who modeled for me what my new identity was to be. They mediated the Franciscan charism for me, and in my choosing their way, Dad's way was to a large extent rejected—until now when I am trying to make amends for the pain my Franciscan vocation caused Dad from time to time. "Make amends" may be too strong a phrase. Perhaps "make peace with my own feeling of guilt" is better because Dad came to understand what I needed to do to move away from him. He understood in the end, but I'm sure it was not easy for him.

What I realize most now is the pain and suffering my Franciscan vocation caused both Mother and Dad. I was so young, fourteen years old, when I left them standing at the Greyhound Bus Station in Gallup and traveled Route 66 some fifteen hundred miles to St. Francis Seminary in Cincinnati. Many other boys and girls did the same and more, some leaving their own country and crossing the sea to another land and culture to enter the novitiate of a religious community. A young girl from Singapore, for example, in the 1950s would have left home and made a sea passage to Italy and then taken a train to France, crossed the English Channel to Dover, to make her way to the English novitiate of the missionary nuns whom she had met and was inspired by in Singapore.

Perhaps she would never see her family again, or if she did it would be years later, should she be sent to Singapore as a missionary herself. All of this for the love of Christ and his call in her heart. The young nun began her journey away from her earthly parents in response to a call. A choice—a terrible choice some would see it—was made that caused both pain and joy. It was a choice that depended on great faith in God, trust of one's own inner movement, the hearing of an inner call.

It is a choice still made today. It separates the child from the parent, but it also unites. For, paradoxically, the child who finds his or her own identity in response to an inner call grows closer to the seemingly abandoned parents. In finding your own way in marriage, or religious life, or a single life, you have a true center from which to love more authentically.

When you leave behind those you love in order to follow an inner call, you re-find those you love. You see more clearly that love involves separation, that only in my being uniquely who I am, a separate, autonomous person, can I love you deeply and truly. Symbiosis is not a healthy basis for love, but rather a debilitating dependence that vitiates the very ground of love.

When you follow the movement of your own call, you may seem to others a selfish, or at least self-centered, person who is reaching too hard for some kind of indefinable self-fulfillment. But that is usually not true. You are really trying to find or keep intact the true self from which to love more deeply those who may feel they are being abandoned for some fad that will only bring resentment on all sides.

As I continue this week of fishing and thinking not only of Dad but of God, who gave him and Mother to me, my love for my parents deepens, intensifies, as it has from the time of my leaving home as a young teenager and removing to a seminary fifteen hundred miles away from them.

It was Saint Francis of Assisi and his response to God that inspired me to leave home in order to listen more attentively to what I believed was my calling. His response has proven to be the right one for me, but I only know that because I did leave, did try to listen, did pass through years of not knowing who I was even when I was doing what I thought I was supposed to do in order to find myself. I did finally reach some kind of centered identity and in that new center I love my parents even more deeply in the love of the One who is the source of all love.

These few pages have brought us, as all word-journeys inevitably do, a long way from the fly-fishing they began with. They have brought us to sons and fathers, to separation that is really further union and, yet, isn't that what the account of my vocation is really about? Didn't I, in embracing my whole self, embrace again the father I tried to leave when I went in search of my soul? And isn't fly-fishing a way of making tangible my own return to my father?

Every returned fish is fish held onto, every kept fish a lost fish. Of such stuff is life—metaphor and paradox. What we give back, lives.

NOTES

[1] Ernest Hemingway, *The Nick Adams Stories* (New York: Charles Scribner's Sons, 1972), pp. 177–178.

Navajo Sheepherder

He came first to St. Michael's Mission, and I remember feeling how ironic was his insistence that he was simply a Navajo sheepherder, given his slow, wise and almost perfectly articulated English. His name was Murray Lincoln. His bearing was that of a medicine man, an unmistakable authority in the way he spoke and moved, though at the same time he was a listener, humble in the way he would always wait for me to finish whatever I was saying, then pause for what seemed an unnaturally long time before responding. He gave the impression that he was genuinely considering everything I'd said, which he was. He wanted to know what I was writing, and he invited me to his hogan so that I could experience firsthand what it was like to be inside a hogan and to converse there in what to him was a sacred space of family and Navajo values. I still have my notes of that visit and that conversation, and this is how it went.

We sat together in his hogan, the sun from the smoke-hole in the center of the roof falling onto my lap. His wife with her gentle, quiet manner was at the woodstove making us a cup of coffee. I remember talking to him about how hard it was to write and make things and people come alive and how I felt so inept to write about the Navajo people. He paused and said, "Yes, the word that falls on paper suddenly stops breathing." That was the way he talked, the sort of thing he would say.

He said that other people before me had come to his hogan and some would even stay in the guest hogan he pointed out to me. He told of one person, a woman from back east, trying to "find herself." Murray Lincoln told her she was welcome to stay for as long as she liked in the hogan next to his and his wife's, "provided," he said, "you are not afraid of a good night's sleep." Not knowing what he meant, the woman decided to stay—she stayed in fact all summer—but told Murray she was an early riser and would join him for coffee early the next morning. She woke up at noon the next day, puzzled, embarrassed, but renewed in a way she'd not been for a long time. Not many words were said all summer, but she continued to sleep well and left in the fall somehow whole and at peace.

Now here we were again at Klagetoh, Arizona, not in his hogan as before, but in the friary next to the mission church. It was evening, and I was working on a manuscript, distracted and preoccupied with whether or not I'd be able to find the Navajo sheepherder, Murray Lincoln, wondering if he was still alive, when there was a knock on the door, and there he stood, asking for his mail, not recognizing me. It had, after all, been almost twenty years. But then he said, "I remember you. We talked. Since then I have had another idea." I invited him in, but he said, "No, we would be rushed. I will come tomorrow morning, ten o'clock."

And that is how it happened, that new encounter with the extraordinary man whom I had remembered off and on for all the intervening years and whom I wanted so much to see again.

Next morning, as I anticipated, he arrived an hour late—according to my watch, which he had dismissed the first time we talked, as superfluous and even dangerous. "You have a wristwatch," he'd said, "but we Navajos have time."

I'd not forgotten those words, having experienced again and again how clocks and watches so often deprive us of time, make us anxious, surround prayer and meditation and conversation with a mechanical measurement that says, "That's enough. You're wasting time," or "You don't have time for this," when what they are really saying is, "We are counting, putting parameters around your prayer, your conversation with God. You have no time for what transpires outside of time."

I knew our conversation would last as long as it took for him to tell me his new idea. I knew I dared not look at my wristwatch or suggest that I had something to *do* later that would rush us or make me say, "I have to go now." We were entering Navajo time, sacred time, not measurable and not to be cut off by a chronological measuring device called (accurately) a watch. We were entering something akin to a ceremony, a liturgy of sorts, the dimension of story-telling and sacred action.

"When Jesus appeared to his apostles after the Resurrection and said, 'Peace be with you,' he was able to give them peace because he himself had acquired it through the sacred ceremony of his passion, death and resurrection. He had attained what we Navajos call *hozhooji*."

Hozhooji is one of the most sacred words of the Navajo people. It means, "the blessed way" and, according to Murray Lincoln, it is attained by fulfilling the sacred ceremonies of life. "The Mass," he said, "is the reenactment of the ceremonies in which Jesus attained *hozhooji*. We need to live the Mass. It is *the* ceremony for attainment of *hozhooji*. Tell that to your brother priests. Tell them to explain the ceremony they are performing. How does that ceremony work? How can we live our lives according to that ceremony? That's what we need. If we do that, we will attain *hozhooji*. Tell them their grandfather, Murray Lincoln, said that."

And so I'm telling the story. Not just to my fellow priests, but to whomever will listen. I asked Murray Lincoln where he got his new thought since I saw him last.

"I was remembering how I became a Catholic. I went to Phoenix as a young boy to visit another boy, my friend, who was attending Brophy, the Jesuit high school there. I went to Mass with him, and as soon as I walked into church, I knew a sacred ceremony was being performed because I heard the Gregorian chant. It was holy. It reminded me of what I felt when I heard the Navajo chant. I wanted to know more about this ceremony, so when I came back home, I asked my parents if I could go to the Catholic boarding school at St. Michaels, Arizona, in the fall. And that's how it happened that I started school at St. Michaels with the Sisters of the Blessed Sacrament.

"Every morning we went to Mass with the sisters. The mother superior sat up in front, and I would watch her praying during the ceremony, especially when the priest lifted the bread and the cup after the Consecration. Her whole face seemed illumined. I would look at what appeared to be bread and a gold cup and then I would look at her. She must have been seeing something else because her face lit up like the sun was shining on it. I knew it had something to do with this ceremony. I wanted to know how to make my face shine like hers. And so I asked to take instructions in the Catholic faith—because of that ceremony that changed the face of the mother superior. That was Mother Katherine Drexel. She is Blessed Katherine Drexel today. The church also saw the light in her face. The church understood the power of Jesus' ceremony in her life. She had reached *hozhooji*."

I said nothing. We paused together for a long time.

I never saw Murray Lincoln again, though I keep his picture on my desk. He died in 1995. But before he died he was privileged to be the final redactor of the Navajo translation of the Mass, now officially approved by the Holy See.

While working on these pages, I journeyed to St. Michaels again and visited Paul Lincoln, Murray's son who is a Navajo medicine man. He told me a story about his father that is the kind of story I'd come to expect from Murray Lincoln.

"My father, Murray Lincoln, came from a long line of traditional medicine men. His father and his father's father before him were medicine men. But for some reason he couldn't come up with the right reasons to become a medicine man himself. Luckily, his father saw something in Murray that called for an education. He wanted him to go away and become educated. So he told his son, 'You can always come back. And remember, a Navajo carries with him his sacred mountains wherever he goes.' Murray wasn't sure what that meant so his father showed him his fist with its four knuckles and named each one of them after one of the sacred mountains. That's what I mean,' he said."

Each time he would look at his hand, he would hear his father's words, and he could, if he wanted, enter each knuckle and pray there on his own sacred mountain. As Murray Lincoln once said so poignantly, "An arrowhead is not a good luck charm. There are prayers that are given to you with it. You are being entrusted with a spirit that is good and that sees your well-being as important. Prayer and song accompanies this object. When you learn how to use it, to pray with it, you find out there is a presence within it."

Some Days the Hogan Is Cold

I have lit cedar and pinon wood in the stove that sits just to the right of the entrance to the octagonal hogan. I've come here to this house of prayer staffed by three Catholic nuns because this chapel of theirs is a converted hogan that reminds me of Murray Lincoln's hogan near Klagetoh. In the center is the traditional smoke hole, but it is glassed over, a skylight through which on this freezing December day the Arizona sunlight streams heatless.

In the wall opposite the traditional eastward-facing entrance the Blessed Sacrament is reserved behind a pine door, and on the floor before the tabernacle rests an Advent wreath with four candles. To the left of the wreath, resting on a sheepskin is the Holy Bible and two eagle feathers, next to which a corn stalk and pollen lie nestled in a conch.

Draped over five benches, in a riot of color, are Navajo blankets, their stripes running east to west according to Navajo custom. A green blanket with red, orange and yellow stripes; a purple blanket with green, red, black and blue stripes; a non-striped blanket with gray, black, red and green symbols; a pink blanket with green and yellow stripes. The floor, unlike the traditional dirt floor of the hogan, is covered with wall-to-wall carpet.

Cedar trees circle the hogan. It is silent here, except for the fire, which is now beginning to crackle and pop. Brother Fire, Saint Francis dubbed it, that mysterious, ambiguous force that both warms and consumes, enlightens and destroys. All seems perfect for prayer, except that the fire isn't doing anything to warm the hogan. It pops and even sounds like it is roaring, but there's no heat, and I move closer to the stove, open the door, pretend it's a fireplace or open fire. I decide to put my cap on, even though I'm in the chapel—memories of virulent colds caught in drafty, chilly churches of Italy impel me to zip up my coat as well.

I sit by the fire thinking only of when it might warm up. I notice patches of rainbow-colored light on the carpet—my eyes move to the crystals hanging in two of the windows. Movement outside the window. Four Navajo horses and two ponies are sauntering by. The wind whips up—I see it in the horses' manes.

And so it goes for over an hour. I thought I would pray so well here. Instead I spend the whole time conscious only of the cold, the stove weak against the chill, the crystals, the light that does not warm, the horses that keep circling the hogan—things I'd not have noticed were I rapt in prayer, inside somewhere, surrendering to the mystery.

But this, too, is prayer. This awareness of what lies about me, of the gift of horses and hogan, stove and crystals and shifting rainbows on the carpet. I've surrendered to the world around me, and my interior calms down, my muscles, despite the cold, begin to relax. I lean back and begin to praise God in the words my father, Saint Francis, gave me.

> Most High, all powerful, good Lord,
> Yours is the praise, the glory and the honor,
> And every blessing.
> They belong to you alone,
> And no one is worthy to speak Your Name.
>
> So, praised be You, My Lord, with all Your creatures,
> Especially Sir Brother Sun,
> Who makes the day and enlightens us through You.
> He is lovely and radiant and grand;
> And he heralds You, his Most High Lord.
>
> Praised be You, my Lord, for Sister Moon
> And for the stars.
> You have hung them in heaven shining and precious
>   and fair,
>
> And praise to You, my Lord, through Brother Wind,
> In air and cloud, and every weather
> Through which You sustain Your creatures.
>
> Praised be You, my Lord, in Sister Water,
> So very useful, humble, precious, and chaste.

Yes, and praise to You, my Lord, for our Sister, Mother
    Earth,
Who nourishes us and teaches us,
Bringing forth all kinds of fruits and colored flowers
    and herbs.[1]

The hogan is still cold, though the stove is beginning to warm. The sunlight is more light than heat, the crystals turn in the draft. My brief prayer is over. I walk out into the bright Arizona noon, a rush of cold air on my face. I shiver—the hogan was warmer than I thought. I see and hear more clearly the crows and horses and the cedar trees bending in the wind, the smoke curling from the hogan's stovepipe. Once again, the prayer that happened, the prayer surrendered to, was better than the one I'd hoped for.

NOTES

[1] Murray Bodo, *Through the Year with Francis of Assisi* (Cincinnati: St. Anthony Messenger Press, 1993), pp. 168–169.

Landscape and Soul

For me, one of the strongest images of the "door" of prayer, the "door" to prayer is Canyon de Chelley in the heart of the Navajo Nation. I come here following my father's death because it is a place where as a boy some fifty years ago my parents would take me. A place of heights, depths, desert, water.

Canyon de Chelley. You look over a ledge and your imagination plummets headlong into a world thousands of years old. Stratum by stratum your gaze falls into the canyon below, its few sheep so distant the sound of their bells rings only in memory.

You come to what looks like a usual overlook, and the world opens up, a huge gash in the earth. It is smaller, yet to me more ragged, mysterious, than the Grand Canyon. The silence of this earth wound repels at first, frightens the unsuspecting traveler. You long for sound, but there is none. Even the beating of a hawk's wings is muffled in the sea of air from canyon wall to canyon wall. Movement without sound. Sound too distant to hear. Unrelenting heat.

Below, like a giant stalagmite, Spider Rock thrusts skyward, as if the world of earth were trying to pierce the sky, to become one with air and cloud and rainbow. This is holy ground. Now, as ever, the same.

Imagine a journey that mirrors an inward journey into silence and solitude. You stand as at here in Canyon de Chelley and look in wonder at something outside of you that opens something similar within. Outer landscape becomes the landscape of your soul, and you long to descend, ledge by ledge, into the canyon cleft. You enter what you fear is a deep void within, but find there instead your own rock, the center from which you came, the center that defines who you are. We can call this inner landscape our soul, we may name it awareness or center or still point, but we recognize it as the place of prayer. And ultimately no matter where we go, we can enter this place, for it is within.

Sometimes, we discover places of paradox: in the midst of the desert, a pool of water; in the full well, the empty cistern. The desert we are fleeing in order to be filled up again may itself be the place of filling; a place of absence may be a place of presence in a way we've not experienced before.

I become more aware of earth, water, air and fire. I befriend them, let God speak through them. The air of my own breathing and the sound of water calm me, the sun's fire warms my whole being, solid earth to walk upon gives me a sense of stability, of strength. These images from nature speak to us of what is happening in the soul. Storms are never just storms; they are metaphors for storms of the soul. And in caring for our soul, we are caring for the body as well, because we are a unity, one person inner and outer, spiritual and physical. The body is not some outer shell that houses the soul; soul and body are one person, the soul giving life to the body, the body incarnating the soul. We recognize that the four elements are not wholly external to the soul, but find their complementarity in the images that rise into our consciousness from the universe within. Our soul's geography is a reflection of the external world, and every landscape we love, as someone once wrote, is the landscape of our soul.

PART SIX:

The Face of God

Sacred Space

I t is an early April morning just after daybreak. I am alone in my room, wanting to read the newspaper or go downstairs and turn on a morning TV show, talk to someone, read about prayer, God, how to write—anything but just sit here and wait for God to move within me. What if—as usual—nothing happens? Does that mean there is no God, that what I keep writing about is really a charade? Won't God come to me, if God comes at all, whether or not I sit or kneel or stand and simply wait expectantly for a divine visitation?

I know from experience that if I don't sit down and write, no matter what else I'd rather be doing, the writing doesn't get done. Nothing just happens spontaneously, a visitation of the muse out of the heavens uttering words that I, like a mechanical scribe, simply copy onto the page. Writing is a process that involves nothing more nor less than putting words down on the page or the computer screen day after day, week after week, month after month, year after year. The inspiration comes because I am writing, not in order that I might transcribe the inspiration. The muse comes to those who dwell in the house of the muse, those who work at their craft day in and day out.

The same is true of prayer. Every day I need to retire to a sacred space within and without and wait there in open expectation. But unlike the act of writing, I don't have to *do* anything but withdraw into that space where I can be open to God's movement within me.

I say "sacred space within and without" because it is important to have a physical, as well as a psychological space, congenial to prayer. It can be a space in my own room, a corner, a nook, a desk or shrine, a window, a place on the floor where I unroll a rug as a prayer mat. It could be the rug itself, which I take with me wherever I travel, thereby sanctifying any space where I choose to unroll my holy rug. Maybe it is a statue or amulet that is portable, like the prayer rug or the writer's notebook and pen.

I am reminded of a memoir of Graham Greene by the writer/editor Michael Korda that appeared in *The New Yorker,* March 25, 1996. Theirs was a friendship that began on Korda's father's yacht, *Elsewhere*, when Michael was sixteen:

> An early riser, he appeared on deck at first light, found a seat in the shade of an awning, and took from his pocket a small black leather notebook and a black fountain pen, the top of which he unscrewed carefully. Slowly, word by word, without crossing out anything, and in neat, square handwriting, the letters so tiny and cramped that it looked as if he were attempting to write the Lord's Prayer on the head of a pin, Graham wrote, over the next hour or so, exactly five hundred words. He counted each word according to some arcane system of his own, and then screwed the cap back onto his pen, stood up and stretched and, turning to me, said, "That's it, then. Shall we have breakfast?" I did not, of course, know that he was completing *The End of the Affair*, the controversial novel based on his own tormenting love affair, nor did I know that the manuscript would end, typically, with an exact word count (63,162) and the time he finished it (August 19th, 7:55 A.M., aboard *Elsewhere*).

When I read that description of Graham Greene writing, it became another image of writing and of prayer. I saw myself writing in like circumstances (minus the yacht and celebrities) all over the United States, in Europe, in England and Ireland. I saw myself praying that way, as well. For me, as a Franciscan and Catholic priest, the Roman Franciscan breviary is my prayer book. I try to open it and pray in it and from it as carefully as Greene unscrewed the cap of his fountain pen and opened his leather notebook and began writing a set number of words, no matter what the external circumstances.

And probably most of us, like Greene, have to force ourselves out of bed before others rise in order to have the kind of quiet time we need for prayer and reflection, for simply waiting for God.

For the prayer the waiting is all. After reading the set prayers and lessons of the breviary, I sit and wait with open heart and mind for something beyond my own desires, my own expectations, my own need to connect with the divine. Like Madame Defarge in Dickens's *A Tale of Two Cities*, who sat and knitted and saw nothing, I sit and wait and see nothing. For my eyes are either turned inward or fixed upon some object that becomes a means of focus rather than of close observation.

I mean, for example, that the candle I look at is not an object to analyze, classify, define, observe with a clinical or image-making eye. The candle is simply something to stare at blankly while being totally receptive and open to whatever comes from the candle or from elsewhere in my consciousness. I'm looking but not necessarily seeing. I'm looking while remaining simultaneously open to the daydream that takes me elsewhere. I'm like someone abstracted in the presence of another who looks at me and says, "A penny for your thoughts." Except, I'm not thinking at all. I'm just there waiting, letting any images that will rise into my consciousness, letting any blankness be just blankness, emptiness. I'm doing nothing, especially nothing productive. I'm letting go of my need to feel in charge, to know, to make or do, to consume or control. I'm in the sacred space of prayer, the *templum,* the "temple," that is in the center of the word *con-templ-ation.*

What happens there cannot be adequately communicated. All I can utter is, "Ah!" So that my whole response to this seemingly useless exercise of setting aside time to sit or kneel or stand in the presence of God, is at some point to utter an inner, "Ah!" in *awe* and gratitude.

Most of the time there is no "ah." There is only the silence, the sense that I am wasting time. But if I remain in the *templum,* the sacred inner and outer space of prayer, something happens to elicit an "ah!" That moment of recognition, of enlightenment, of grace is the reason I keep coming back in gratitude for the otherwise inexpressible, in anticipation that it will happen again if I submit myself to the surrender and discipline of prayer.

Of course, something has to change outside the space and time of prayer if I am going to continue experiencing the gift of prayer's illumination. We need to change our lives or prayer will become a dangerous, addictive drug that is more an escape from life than a transformation of life. Prayer then becomes as addictive as whatever happens to be the latest compulsive fad, from working out to dieting to jogging. The prayer I enter every day is not for the "ah," but for the transformation of my life that prayer's illumination invites me to. And that transformation is not just for my own self-fulfillment or gratification or, worse, for self-aggrandizement. It is for charity, for the transformation of the world I live in through my charity rather than my self-righteous judgments or self-satisfied pose of having attained something others don't have.

If others see anything different in me, it will no doubt be a new-found joy and delight in them and in the world around me, rather than a subtle superiority that sets me apart or above as some kind of "enlightened one." I become more aware of others, more compassionate and understanding and certainly less judgmental. There is no more affirming feeling than to be loved by a saint. And a saint is one who has spent time daily in *con-templ-ation* and followed through on each revelatory experience.

Each of us can become a saint by praying, just as each of us can become a writer by writing. Maybe not a great saint or a great writer, but a saint and writer just the same who has had his or her "ah" experiences simply because we stuck with the discipline of prayer or writing.

Now, I've written all this, and it is still morning, and I'm still here in the April indoor and outdoor weather, and I didn't know where I was because I was in the words. Now I notice again where I am. I close my notebook. I screw my pen cap closed. I begin my day away from pen and notebook, which I nevertheless take with me and return to during the day to read what I wrote, to ask myself what I should do about what I wrote.

Surely, one thing I need to do is write again tomorrow. Maybe I'll even just sit and pray in *con-templ-a-tion before* I write. Looks like I need to do more than write *about* prayer. Guess I'll have to give in and do what I'm suggesting you need to do. Words do make us responsible, call us to stand by them.

The Face of God

To behold the face of God. Or, if that is not possible, to find the icon of God's countenance in what I can see. This is the deepest desire of one who believes in God as a separate, transcendent, yet immanent being. This same desire is why one enters into prayer: to find the face of God or to find the means whereby to see God's face revealed in one's ordinary, day-to-day life.

But what is the true face of God, and can we be deceived into thinking we are seeing the face of God when it is really the face of our own illusions? The Gospel story of Christ's forty days in the desert lights our way.

Led by the Spirit, Jesus went out into the desert to be tempted by the devil, who is ever intent on deceiving us into thinking that his face is really the face of God. Jesus went into the desert to see and reject once and for all the false faces of God, in order to embrace the true face of God and reveal that face to everyone who would see. And so Jesus, the model of the person of prayer, goes out into the desert to fast and pray for forty days—an allusion to the forty days the Hebrew people wandered in the desert seeking the face of God—and to be alone, in silence, with the desert creatures. Then, only after these forty intensely spiritual days, did Satan tempt Jesus with the false faces of God. For it is often after we have immersed ourselves intensely in spiritual practice (as in the Christian tradition of fasting for the forty days of Lent) that we are most vulnerable to temptation, being then open to the spiritual world in a way we are not when we are preoccupied with materialities.

As the Gospel of Luke tells the story, Jesus "ate nothing at all during those days, and when they were over, he was famished. The devil said to him, 'If you are the Son of God, command this stone to become a loaf of bread.' Jesus answered him, 'It is written, "One does not live by bread alone"'" (Luke 4:2–4). The first false face of God: God is the one who is able to provide food and nourishment to the hungry, as if the satisfying of bodily hunger will feed the deep hunger of the soul.

God provided food in the form of manna in the desert between Egypt and the Promised Land, but the manna did not make the people more spiritual. It merely sustained their bodily lives and set up the expectation that God's face is the face of the Provider. So that, if I am not provided for, if I am hungry and without food, God has abandoned me, or I am not worthy, or worse, there is no God. The one who is well fed and prosperous, then, is the one who is the image of God. Food and prosperity become signs of God's presence and God's blessing. But Jesus rejects this face as false: "One does not live by bread alone."

The second temptation follows hard on the first and presents a face of Power, as does the first temptation: "Then the devil led him up and showed him in an instant all the kingdoms of the world. And the devil said to him, 'To you I will give their glory and all this authority, for it has been given over to me, and I will give it to anyone I please. If you, then, will worship me, it will all be yours.' Jesus answered him, 'It is written, "Worship the Lord your God and serve only him"'" (Luke 4:5–8). Dominion and glory—power, in other words—is the second false face of God.

A story is told of an old Franciscan friar in Holland who, a few years before he died, made an extraordinary statement. "The trouble with the modern world," he said, "is that it no longer knows the secret of the spiritual life." His interlocutor, himself a friar, was of course eager to know from his saintly confrere what the forgotten secret was and waited anxiously to hear it from the aged friar who paused long and effectively, as good storytellers do, before looking up and saying, "The secret is this: we moderns look for God where there is power and God is revealed in powerlessness." Actually, he said, "And God is powerless," but I in retelling the story related the meaning rather than the words and then felt guilty doing so, both because that is not what the old friar said and because my editing presumes that the reader could misunderstand the original words. And so I control their implication, thereby in one sentence appropriating to myself the power which I claim in the same paragraph is not God. I fall into the very trap I am warning against.

Again and again we fall into the trap of power as being God-like. But if power is the face of God, then the most powerful ruler is the image of God. Jesus says, rather, "Worship the Lord your God, and serve only him." The face of God is revealed in adoration, not in power. Once you adore, you acknowledge that you are not God-like in being powerful but in bowing before the mystery of a being who *Is* rather than who *Does*. "I *am* the LORD your God," the first commandment reads, "you shall not have strange gods before me" (Exodus 20:2–3).

Then "the devil took [Jesus] to Jerusalem and placed him on the pinnacle of the temple, saying, 'If you are the Son of God, throw yourself down from here; for it is written [Jesus had been using Scripture so now Satan does], "He will command his angels concerning you, to protect you" and "On their hands they will bear you up, so that you will not dash your foot against a stone."' Jesus answered him, 'It is said, "Do not put the Lord your God to the test"'" (Luke 4:9–12).

No matter what, the tempter suggests, God will take care of me. I can be foolhardy, I can take risks; God will keep me safe. God cares for his own. This final false face is perhaps the most difficult to let go of. We cannot understand how God can stand by and let so many atrocities happen. This temptation is closely tied to the previous one wherein we insist that God is power and acts incessantly in our behalf. Some latch onto Jesus' own words,

> Look at the birds of the air; they neither sow nor reap nor gather into barns, and yet your heavenly Father feeds them. Are you not of more value than they? And can any of you by worrying add a single hour to your span of life? And why do you worry about clothing? Consider the lilies of the field, how they grow: they neither toil nor spin, yet I tell you even Solomon in all his glory was not clothed like one of these. But if God so clothes the grass of the field, which is alive today, and tomorrow is thrown into the oven, will he not much more clothe you—you of little faith? (Matthew 6:26–30)

But when we look at what Jesus asks us to look at, we see that lilies wither and die; they are picked prematurely; they are crowded out by weeds. And the birds of the air are shot from the sky by hunters; they starve; they are the prey of other animals. What are we to make of this? Are Jesus' words simply sentimental, sweet-sounding music, or is something other being said? Jesus himself is abandoned by his Father and left to die upon a cross, so he is not being naive in asking us to consider the lilies of the field, the birds of the air.

God's face is not that of the Doer but of the Lover. God is love, as Saint John the Evangelist reminds us. The difference between us and the lilies and birds is not that nothing untoward ever happens to them, but that they don't worry about it the way we do. We are anxious and worry, as if worrying itself will do something to prevent the inevitable, to lessen the pain, to stop death.

The face of God is not that of the Protector against all harm, but of the Lover of all that is, who, no matter what happens to us, loves us with an unchangeable, unconditional love. And we misunderstand love when we put it to the test by insisting that if it doesn't keep us from all harm, then it is not love. Loves saves by loving, not by protecting. What we know of God in the end is not that we will never suffer injury or death, but that no matter what happens, we will be ever in God's loving embrace. God will clothe us with his love, even if like the grass we are thrown naked into the oven.

The truest face of God is love. That is the ultimate knowledge that prayer imparts. The prayer at some point—maybe after years of praying—emerges at last with only the first words of Jesus after his sojourn in the desert: "The time is fulfilled, and the kingdom of God is near. Repent and believe in the good news" (Mark 1:15). These words are *the* lesson prayer: If I repent (change my point of view, my heart, my orientation), I will see that the kingdom of God is indeed near. It is all around me and within me when I understand at last what it means that God is simply—love.

The Eye of the Heart

"T he eye of the heart." How different that is from "the mind." For knowing something intellectually does not necessarily change our heart or our behavior. I can know I'm in sin or messed up or addicted, and at the same time maintain a curious detachment from any need to change. Something has to happen in the "heart," that mysterious word we use and associate almost automatically with some deep center within which is the source of good and evil, the dwelling place of the most essential self that is almost another person with its own eye for seeing, its own ears for hearing, its own will for perpetrating good and/or evil. And yet we know "heart" is not separate from us, dwelling in us like another "I."

The heart is that in me which is me at my most centered and essential self. Biblically, the heart is the locus of our conscious activity of intellect and will. It is where we know we know and know what we're doing or failing to do. The heart's seeing is connected to acting or failing to act. The eye of the heart, then, is not just consciousness. It is conscience. And conscience is cleansed, according to Saint Bernard, when we begin praying, "Heal me, O God, and I shall be healed; save me and I shall be saved," and "O God, be gracious to me, for I have sinned against you."

In a sermon that compresses prayer into a few deft lines, Saint Bernard writes, "We are troubled when we contemplate ourselves, and our sorrow brings salvation; when we contemplate God we are restored, so that we receive consolation from the joy of the Holy Spirit. From the contemplation of ourselves we gain fear and humility; but from the contemplation of God, hope and love."[1]

Saint Bernard teaches that the first step in prayer is to contemplate God. From that contemplation we are led to ask, what does God want? What is God's will? What is pleasing and acceptable in God's sight? But as soon as we try to answer these kinds of questions, we realize how far we are from God, how removed from any real knowledge of who God is, let alone what

God wants. We become aware, too, of our own sins and mistakes and our need for mercy. We've offended Someone, some Love-Power, some All-Goodness in the universe, and we are moved to cry out, "Heal me, O God, and I shall be healed; save me and I shall be saved" and "O God, be gracious to me, heal me, for I have sinned against you."

Saint Bernard then makes an important observation: "Once the eye of our heart has been cleansed by dwelling on thoughts of this kind, we are no longer left in bitterness in our own spirit, but we have great joy in the Spirit of God." How much is here, how keenly said.

What *could* lead to discouragement, self-hatred or at least to a poor self-image does not. In fact, "by dwelling on thoughts of this kind we are no longer left in bitterness in our own spirit, but we have great joy in the Spirit of God." Why is that? For one thing, the very articulation of "O God, be gracious to me, heal me," is the heart's acknowledgment that there *is* someone out there or in me who is greater than I, who can grant mercy, who can forgive. Only "the eye of the heart" can see this truth and act on it. Only "the eye of the heart" has vision enough to change its seeing: to see that I am not my own universe, my own self-sufficient world. Someone made me, someone saved me, someone cares about me and sustains me. As Julian of Norwich succinctly puts it:

> And [the Lord] showed me . . . a little thing, the size of a hazelnut, on the palm of my hand, round like a ball. I looked at it thoughtfully and wondered, "what is this?" And the answer came, "It is all that is made." I marveled that it continued to exist and did not suddenly disintegrate; it was so small. And again my mind supplied the answer, "It exists both now and forever, because God loves it." In short, everything owes its existence to the love of God.
>
> In this "little thing" I saw three truths. The first is that God made it; the second is that God loves it; and the third is that God sustains it. But what he is who is in truth Maker, Keeper, and Lover I cannot tell, for until I am essentially united with him I can never have full rest or real happiness; in other words, until I am so joined to him that there is absolutely nothing

between my God and me. We have got to realize the littleness of creation and see it for the nothing that it is before we can love and possess God who is un-created.[2]

The cry of the heart, "O God, be gracious to me, heal me," is the beginning of the change of heart that ultimately surrenders in love to the love who is Love. And bitterness dissolves like the ice it is without love's warmth. Bitterness is hatred turned inward because there is nowhere for it to go, no way to strike out, or change someone else, or remedy a bad situation in ourselves or others. But when we begin to see (with "the eye of the heart") God and God's mercy and love, we begin to change, so that no matter how great is the real or imagined evil "out there," we are letting go of its hold on us and letting God hold us, forgive us, love us. This, then, is joy, is the Spirit of God: God's indwelling, God's inrush into the open heart, the heart that asks for God's entry.

Saint Bernard then adds, "We do not now consider what is God's will for us, but what God's will is, in itself." Which is what happens when we cease referring everything to ourselves, as if we were the measure and judge of all, as if all were made for us. To know God's will in itself is to know pure goodness. As Julian of Norwich writes,

> To know the goodness of God is the highest prayer of all, and it is a prayer that accommodates itself to our most lowly needs. . . . [God] does not despise the work of his hands, nor does he disdain to serve us, however lowly our natural need may be. . . . For just as the body is clothed in its garments, and the flesh in its skin, and the bones in their flesh, and the heart in its body, so too are we, soul and body, clothed from head to foot in the goodness of God.[3]

We are clothed in the goodness of God. That sentence, that truth, is where the contemplation of God ultimately leads. And the re-alization of what does indeed clothe us is the source of the hope and love and joy that Saint Bernard claims for the contempla-tive. Whatever the prayer, if it does not lead ultimately to the contemplation of God, it will not bring us true hope and love and joy. These three gifts are the barometer of the heart's communing with God.

Now, easy does it. The way to hope and love and joy is not in a quick prayer. It may involve many prayers with a residue of hopelessness, bitterness and sadness. For the way to God is through the heart and there may be a lot of inner work to be done before we're really contemplating God and not ourselves in a divine guise. But even as we make what may be an arduous heart-journey to God, there will be peace along the way, some assurance that we are on the right path. We will get glimpses of hope, love and joy, and those sightings keep us coming back to our prayer into the heart through whose eye alone we contemplate God.

Every prayer, then, is really an entering into our deep heart's core—whether we are contemplating nature, art or people. Then, through the heart's eye we see God in nature, art and other people, all of which have become God's countenance.

NOTES

[1] *The Divine Office* (London and Glasgow: Collins, 1974), pp. 522–523.
[2] Julian of Norwich, *Revelations of Divine Love* (Middlesex, England: Penguin Books, 1966), p. 68.
[3] Ibid., p. 70.

The Evergreen Tree:
Praying with the Dalai Lama

Iam back again at Gethsemani Abbey in the Kentucky hills
near Bardstown. No hermitage this time. Instead, it is all saf-
fron-robed Buddhist monks and nuns, gray-robed Zen monks
and nuns praying and sharing spiritual insights with black-
robed Benedictines and white-and-black robed Cistercian monks
and nuns. I am here to observe and chronicle this extraordinary
experience. I am also here because I am drawn to one person—a
singular Buddhist monk who sits not on a dais as one would expect, but among the assembled monks, one of them, one of us—
yet more. He is His Holiness, the Dalai Lama, spiritual and tem-
poral leader of the Tibetan people. He has come here to
participate in an East-West monastic dialogue. He has come, as
well, to the final resting place of his friend, the Trappist monk,
Thomas Merton.

Merton visited the Dalai Lama for three days in 1968 shortly
before his death in Bangkok, and now in a reciprocal pilgrimage
twenty-eight years later, in the third week of July 1996, the
Dalai Lama walks the rise to Thomas Merton's grave among his
brother Trappists in the grass plot beside the monastery wall.
There His Holiness kneels and prays, saying as he rises from the
ground, "Now our spirits are one. I am at peace."

In this simple gesture is not only the friendship between
Merton and the Dalai Lama, but the power of love and prayer, as
well. For when Merton traveled to the East for the first Asian
East-West Intermonastic Conference in Bangkok, he was searching for the level of prayer where we all come together as human
beings. In his *Asian Journal* Merton writes, "I think that we
have now reached a stage of (long overdue) religious maturity at
which it may be possible for someone to remain perfectly faithful
to a Christian and Western monastic commitment and yet learn
in depth from, say, a Buddhist or Hindu discipline or experience."[1] And after meeting the Dalai Lama at Dharmsala, India,

the seat of the Tibetan government-in-exile, Merton wrote to his abbot, Dom Flavian Burns, "The talks with the Dalai Lama were very fine. He did a lot of off the record talking, very open and sincere, a very impressive person, deeply concerned about the contemplative life, and also very learned. I have seldom met anyone with whom I clicked so well, and I feel that we have become great friends."[2]

And so they had. For here in the midst of this dialogue and retreat, it is evident to everyone that the Dalai Lama maintains a deep affection for his friend Thomas Merton. He credits Merton with opening his eyes to the truth that Tibetan Buddhism does not hold the world's only truth. "As a result of my meeting with Thomas Merton," he says,

> my perception and attitude toward Christianity was much improved, much changed. So I always consider him as a strong bridge to Christianity. His sudden death was a great loss. We must try to fulfill his wishes, and I think here we are fulfilling one of his great wishes. . . . This is very helpful, for we are not here to advertise our own religion. There is no competition, except in implementation; we should compete in implementing in our lives what we believe. I would like to be a better practitioner myself; saying something nice is not of much use compared to implementation.[3]

And implementation there is at this Gethsemani encounter. There is much prayer and silence, much reverent breathing in of the thoughts and words of others, much exhaling of what is alien and divisive. The atmosphere is cordial and friendly and the schedule monastic.

For many the high point of the Dalai Lama's presence is the interfaith ritual in the abbey church in memory of Thomas Merton. It is led by Dom James Conner, Cistercian Abbot of Assumption Abbey at Ava, Missouri, who lived with Merton at Gethsemani. Thomas Merton, Conner says, "came to recognize that the East has something which we in the West tend to overlook or neglect." The Dalai Lama says, "Thomas Merton is someone we can look up to. He had the qualities of being learned, disciplined and having a good heart." Then His Holiness places zinnia blossoms around a picture of Merton on a table in front of the choir podium. He places a white shawl about the picture, then offers as a present to abbot Timothy Kelly of Gethsemani a silver chalice containing an orange—because an empty chalice is not proffered as a gift, and the orange is at hand, round and beautiful and as good as any gift the chalice could contain. Abbot Timothy gives the Dalai Lama three recently published volumes of Thomas Merton's journals.

Simple gestures like these abound during this retreat, beginning with Abbot Timothy and the Dalai Lama planting an evergreen tree and continuing through small acts of kindness between Buddhists and Christians, quiet conversations taking place in corners of the abbey, on hillsides, on patios. And every day there are vans taking participants to Thomas Merton's hermitage a short distance from the abbey. His simple, cinder-block hermitage becomes a daily pilgrimage for practically all the participants. Merton has touched everyone here in one way or another. Speakers quote him often, tell stories, cite from his books.

Following the example of Merton, Christians ask Buddhists about methods and practices of prayer; Buddhists ask about the long tradition of social action in the Christian tradition. One Christian participant notes that while Christianity has a long tradition of meditation, it has been obscured by centuries of emphasis on social action and now many Christians are looking to the East to relearn meditation. When asked how he reconciles the apparent conflict between prayer and social action, the Dalai Lama has no easy answer but says he would recommend a "fifty-fifty" split between prayer and action. Buddhists are inclined to withdraw from the world, he says. "We have to learn from our Christian brothers and sisters. We should have more socially engaged activities."

One Buddhist monk who personifies social action among Buddhist monastics is the Venerable Maha Ghosananda, "the Ghandi of Cambodia." This man of peace, who has been nominated three times for the Nobel Peace Prize for his work among Cambodian refugees, says simply,

> We Buddhists must find the courage to leave our temples and enter the temples of human experience, temples that are filled with suffering. If we listen to the

Buddha, Christ or Ghandi, we can do nothing else. The refugee camps, the prisons, the ghettos, and the battlefields will become our temples. We have so much work to do.

This will be a slow transformation, for many people throughout Asia have been trained to rely on the traditional monkhood. Many Cambodians tell me, "Venerable, monks belong in the temple." It is difficult for them to adjust to this new role, but we monks must answer the increasingly loud cries of suffering. We only need to remember that our temple is with us always. We are our temple.

Here in this simple, good man, I hear the very essence of prayer. It is never for us alone; always it implies an entering in, as in breathing in, that necessarily involves a coming out, a breathing out, if there is to be a life-giving balance. We pray and we learn to act with love in the world; we act with love in the world and we learn to pray.

For me and for many others this whole dialogue/retreat has been the search for that place within all of us, named differently in different traditions, where we meet that which is deepest in ourselves and in our tradition and from which we reach out to others in love or, in the language of Buddhism, in loving-kindness. The Dalai Lama himself says, "My religion is kindness." And to those of us who have been privileged to experience his presence, his words are his actions.

At one point of the retreat, unexpectedly and unsought—this is the kind of surprise that sometimes happens on retreat—I find myself, with only a few other participants in the room, very close to His Holiness the Dalai Lama. Something moves me to approach him and ask if we could pray together briefly. Taking my hand, he prays with me in silence, then looks into my eyes with loving-kindness such as I have seldom ever experienced. Such is the effect of compassion; it speaks without words.

This simple, loving gesture touches some deep part of me—it is, in fact the center of the retreat for me. What I came here for I find in the Dalai Lama's eyes, in the warm touch of his hand in mine, in his silent prayer with me. Another person, a person I did not know I would meet personally has made all the difference.

The Dalai Lama tells us the following story of his own experience that reminds me of mine with him.

> On another occasion I met with a Catholic monk in Montserrat, one of Spain's famous monasteries. I was told that this monk had lived for several years as a hermit on a hill just behind the monastery. When I visited the monastery, he came down from his hermitage especially to meet me. As it happened, his English was even worse than mine, and this gave me more courage to speak with him! We remained face to face, and I inquired, "In those few years, what were you doing on that hill?" He looked at me and answered, "Meditation on compassion, on love." As he said those few words, I understood the message through his eyes. I truly developed genuine admiration for this person and for others like him. Such experiences have helped confirm in my mind that all the world's religions have the potential to produce good people, despite their differences of philosophy and doctrine.

Then, through an interpreter, he tells simply and concretely how he meditates on compassion.

> You take in sentient beings who are suffering and you wish them to be free of suffering. And what is love but to take in beings bereft of happiness and wish that they be endowed with happiness? Of course, we can be biased and be worried about someone who likes us and whom we care about deeply. This is not necessarily compassion; it could be attachment. Genuine compassion is there irrespective of another's attitude toward you. Compassion must be unbiased, it must be directed even to your enemy.
>
> Now to develop true compassion is first of all to visualize a being whose level of suffering is such that to our ordinary minds, we feel we can't bear it; we just don't want to look at it. But take that person to mind and reflect on his or her qualities of suffering and then on the similarities with yourself wanting happiness

and not wanting suffering and through that you will feel very strongly a sense of concern for that other person. That is how compassion is developed.

Then move your meditation to other persons, various close persons, one by one, and develop the same sense of concern with respect to them. So that eventually it's important that we take to mind those persons with respect to whom we have a hard time developing compassion. We have to emphasize developing compassion with respect to those beings. In the Gospels also there is the same practice of developing patience, forbearance.

I also want to mention something that is in Buddhist texts that I think is very well understood by our Christian sisters and brothers. This being the cultivation of an altruistic intention to develop oneself for the sake of others and in this process to realize that one has a self-cherishing and a lack of cherishing others and then reflect on the disadvantages and fault of cherishing oneself and the advantages of cherishing others. But this does not mean to neglect your own situation entirely in order to develop a sense of cherishing others. You have to know first what it means to cherish yourself. I do not mean to say one should forget oneself, at all. I am talking about ridding oneself of that selfishness which does not hesitate to exploit or harm another. I am not encouraging low self-esteem or hating yourself; that is sad and not good.

Words like these and their tone of reverence for others, encourage not only the cherishing of others here and their traditions and beliefs and practices, but they encourage self-cherishing, too, and a renewed commitment to our own practices and beliefs. I hear, for example, about prayer techniques, I learn terms like "Nibbana," "Buddha self," "Buddha nature," "loving-kindness." I see good and holy monks and lay people whose Buddhist practices have led them to deep interiority and kindness. I see good and holy monks and lay people whose Christian meditation and contemplation have led them to deep interiority and charity.

The witness of an ecumenical retreat such as this Gethsemani encounter is that we need not give up our own convictions or beliefs, whatever they may be, in order to pray together, talk together in love and kindness. In fact, by adhering with deep faith to our own traditions and yet keeping ever an open heart for all good, we more easily see the good in other traditions.

I see other ways, teachings, rules of life, and sacred rites here at Gethsemani. I turn again to my own, examine the practices, the teachings, the rules and sacred rites that have brought me to this point in my spiritual life. Being here, listening, observing and receiving the loving-kindness of my Buddhist brothers and sisters has enriched me, made me want to learn more about how they pray, what prayer does in their lives. It makes me want to share with them what Christ has done in my life, how he has taught me to pray, what Christian contemplation and meditation have done for me. In short, I am more confident sharing than when I arrived here five days ago, feeling woefully ignorant of Buddhist traditions, feeling intimidated by all the intellectuals and theologians in both traditions, feeling inadequate to write about what I was to observe and record. Now I know the names of many Buddhist brothers and sisters. I've heard them speak; I've seen them pray. And, most importantly, I've experienced their compassion, their loving-kindness reaching out to me and to all their Christian brothers and sisters here and throughout the world. For as one Buddhist monk observed, loving-kindness, like the arms of Jesus on the cross, reaches out and embraces the whole world.

NOTES

[1] Thomas Merton, *Asian Journal of Thomas Merton* (New York: New Directions, 1973), p. 313.
[2] Ibid., p. 178, footnote 39.
[3] Transcribed by author from a talk by the Dalai Lama.

PART SEVEN
Still in the Mystery

Return

When I was thirteen, I reached up and lifted off the shelf of the Gallup Junior High library a small volume entitled *God's Troubadour, the Story of St. Francis of Assisi.* I had lost the title and the author until the summer after my father's death when I was leisurely perusing the card catalogue in the small public library in Millbrook, New York. There it was, the book that meant so much, that changed everything. I could not find it on the shelves, at first, not realizing that it was in juvenilia, a small book by Sophie Jewett, published first in 1910.

No wonder the small volume had touched me so as a boy—its rhythms, the simple Franciscan sentences, the mysterious opening paragraph:

> Under the arched gate of a city wall, a group of people stood watching the road that wound down the mountain and off across the plain. The road lay dusty and white in September sunshine, and the eyes of the watchers followed it easily until it hid itself in a vast forest that filled half the valley. On the point where road and forest met, the sharpest eyes were fixed.[1]

That first reading was in 1950. The following year I left for the seminary. Twenty-two years later, in 1972, I was teaching English at the same seminary and was released from classes during the spring quarter to write a book that involved arcing across the Atlantic to Rome on my way to Assisi to find the gate where the crowd of watchers had waited. Sophie Jewett wrote thus of Assisi.

> Assisi, at whose gate the watchers stood, lies far across the sea in beautiful Italy. It is a little city, built on a mountainside, with a great wall all about it, and a castle on the height above, and it looks very much as it did on that September afternoon more than seven

hundred years ago, when Francis Bernardone waited for his father.[2]

Thus began a journey I repeated summer after summer, searching for my spiritual father, Francis, and now, in order to release my own father and mother to the Italy of their roots.

NOTES

[1] Sophie Jewett, *God's Troubadour, the Story of St. Francis of Assisi* (New York: Thomas Y. Crowell Co., 1910, 1957), p. 1.
[2] Ibid., p. 2.

Geographies

I t is raining softly now, as it was so often during my first time in Assisi. That was in an April and everything in Saint Francis' mystical city seemed soft then like this rain now. La Citta Mistica, "the mystical city." And so it is, every time I retreat in memory, now almost twenty-five years later, to that sacred time and place. That first time was a real place and time, Assisi, 1971. It was also the time of Saint Francis, 1182–1226, and that time was made of words. Early mornings I lived in the words; afternoons and evenings I returned to the world of 1971. At night I dreamed the words I'd read and prayed over.

It was all like play, like a retreat to another time and place my imagination kept taking me. Prayer flowed out of and into leisure and the leisure was born of a relative freedom from attachment to persons and things. My sense of responsibility was focused on prayer and meditation; God was taking care of everyone and everything else whose welfare usually preoccupied me. I began to know what Saint Francis felt in prayer: play and timelessness and intimacy with God.

God was in the room where I lived that spring just as God was in Francis' hermitages, the places of solitude he established up and down Umbria, usually a day's journey apart, thus indicating the basic rhythm of his life: walking the roads of the world by day, retiring at sunset to a mountain hermitage to pray.

Retire. *Retiro*, the Italian word for a hermitage, a place to retire, *re-tirare*, to pull back, to draw back.

But to pull back from what? From the headlong, sometimes headstrong, movement for movement's sake, in order to prolong the illusion that one is going somewhere, when often one is in a labyrinth precipitately taking whatever way is open, whatever road seems to be going somewhere.

The *retiro* of Saint Francis, usually on a mountainside, is a way out of the labyrinth, at least long enough to see that it is a labyrinth one is walking. The perspective of the *retiro* locates road to landscape, to the larger, albeit limited, vision of the whole day's journey. And since to the *retiro*, the retreat, there is a vertical ascent, the soul is alerted to the way of prayer, the longing to rise above, to meet God's hand reaching down to uplift what has become bogged down in plodding along the road.

Usually this ascending is followed by descending. One ascends to enter into the cave of the mountain as into a womb to be born again, just as I ascended Assisi's winding streets to the room where I meditated as into a kind of creative womb where all was gestation and organic growth. And when I descended again to the Piazza del Commune, nothing was the same. Everything seemed charmed somehow, surrounded by the halo of what had happened in my cell. I usually tried to ascend again before the halo wore off.

That rhythm, that dynamic of ascent and descent, of solitary retreat and human commerce, of my room at St. Anthony's Hospice and the Bar Minerva in the Piazza del Commune, I've never regained as consistently and easily as that first April and May in Assisi. The closest I've come is in the brief periods in Assisi with other pilgrims in tow and lots of attachments and emotional baggage weighting me down.

Still, I am not discouraged. That first experience remains inside me, a paradigm of what I need to do to experience anew the freedom and peace and joy of Saint Francis' mystical city. And if I cannot repeat the experience, I can at least retreat into the cave of memory and meditate.

Prayer and action, they call it. I would add, seeing, too. Prayer and seeing and action. A sort of cyclic trinity. I pray therefore I see therefore I act therefore I pray, and so on. And all of this is made visual for me in the circle from St. Anthony's Hospice on the Via Galeazzo Alessi to the Piazza del Commune and thence back by way of the Via Santa Chiara to the steps leading from the Piazza di Santa Chiara to the Via Galeazzo Alessi. A small circle, a huge journey.

Images

Assisi is alive in my heart, my imagination, my dreams. It is a landscape I hold within and to which I escape whenever the pressures or pain of living become too great. And there in that Assisi of the heart I commune again and again with Saint Francis and Saint Clare, with Brother Juniper and all the "fools" of Francis.

I see a flower, a tree, a bowl of pasta that remind me of Italy, and I am off, "off forth on swing," in Gerard Manley Hopkins's marvelous phrase, "as a skate's heel sweeps smooth on a bow bend." Why do I remember that line, whole and beautiful and fixed in my memory like the tiled roofs of Assisi, the curves in the road below the Basilica of St. Francis, the road that leads to Ponte San Giovanni and Perugia? Is it because there is something in my memory of Assisi that sweeps me clean and free, almost off my feet, like the skater in Hopkins's image? Perhaps it is because in Assisi when I first lived there, I was free and happy in a way I'd not been before. I knew who I was, as an American, a Franciscan, a third-generation Italian-American whose parents' roots lay deep in the peasantry of the Piedmont and the Trentino. Turin and Trent, the poles of my roots, one on the border of France, the other on the border of Austria, like my own growing up where New Mexico borders Arizona to the west and Colorado to the north.

Why is it we find ourselves away from home and literally *find* ourselves? I knew in Assisi who I was. And so I long to keep returning, at least in the mind. I retreat in memory, and once again I am in the Casa Papa Giovanni and Suor Ave and Suor Severina and Darinka are there, and Don Aldo and the bishop, and all the pilgrims who came there with us summer after summer. I am in my small second-floor room facing Via San Paolo, from whose stone pavement below I hear the noisy late-night teenagers laughing and singing, their raucous voices ricocheting off the walls of the narrow street and reminding me of the young Francis carousing through the same street with his friends, the songs of the troubadours on his lips, his multi-colored cloak a fit vesture for the King of Revels, as he was often dubbed by his peers.

Images of the Middle Ages flood my mind, and I am standing at another window, this time in St. Anthony's Hospice on the Via Galeazzo Alessi, the morning of my first day in Assisi, stunned and certain I've gone mad as citizens robed in medieval attire walk the streets below. I arrived late the previous night, knowing nothing of the Calendi Maggio, the Calends of May celebration, wherein the Assisians at the beginning of each May don medieval attire and transform with games and contests and song their modern city into the town of Saints Francis and Clare. Only the reassuring, authoritative voice of the sister superior of the hospice convinces me I've not skated round the bend in my enthusiasm and joy at being there in the city of my holy father, Saint Francis.

That, or some similar variation, is how my Assisi meditations begin. It may be early morning. I've just awakened and am already moving faster than I should. I'm going through different scenarios of how I'll approach my 8:30 A.M. freshman comp class. I'm rehearsing what I'll say, if anything, in Writers' Workshop II, a fiction writing or poetry writing workshop that usually does much better when I say nothing, but instead let the students share their writing and talk to each other about it. I'm wondering if I've "lost" my students because of a three-week absence to bury my dad. And how long will I be able to juggle spiritual direction, weekend retreats, teaching, relationships, writing and trying to be present to my brothers?

And then I move to a small alcove in my room where my Assisi mementos are. And I begin, just looking at them, to travel back in time, forward into eternity. And Francis and Clare are there, and they "talk" to me of God, answer my questions or not, depending on whether or not they have anything to say.

The Assisi scenario is one of two meditations that seem never to fail me. The other is made up of memories of the Navajo reservation when I was a boy. Maybe it is simply childhood itself that is the other funding experience we all have and which we can all return to and find there prayer-images enough for a lifetime.

I realize there are those who say prayer, if it is true, must be without images. But I am a Franciscan whose prayer-life is of a tradition formally called *kataphatic*, to differentiate it from the apophatic tradition. The kataphatic tradition uses images, symbols, concepts and ideas to come to God, whereas the apophatic tradition believes that images and ideas get in the way of pure, empty consciousness in which God is more readily experienced.

Following Saint Francis himself, the Franciscan prays and meditates using images from the life of Christ, a method of prayer later articulated more fully by Saint Ignatius Loyola, the founder of the Jesuits.

In the Christian tradition one cannot underestimate the importance of images, given the fact that Christ himself is, in the words of Saint Paul, the image of the living God. Or in Jesus' own words, "I and the Father are One." But the image does not stop with the image. Its dynamic is circular: Christ is the image of the living God, who lives in approachable light, a light made manifest in the Image. God is Image and Imageless, and both truths are involved in the dynamic of prayer. The fullness of prayer, therefore, involves both the kataphatic and the apophatic tradition.

The gestures of a monk, for example, the prostrations, the chanting, the bowing of the head, the closing of the eyes, the folding of the hands, all are images of prayer that prepare the soul for receiving what is essentially imageless.

An example from sleep and dreams may help. Sleep is the place of images. And even if I don't remember them, if I've been dreaming just before waking, I awake with feelings imparted by the images of sleep. I'm happy, frightened, sad, perplexed, hopeful, and so on until I realize it was probably only a dream that caused me to feel like this, and I dismiss it all as part of my dream-life.

The effects of prayer are similar. I come out of prayer, with or without images, with certain inexplicable feelings: contrition, gratitude, awe, peacefulness, though I may have no sense of anything particularly dramatic or divine happening. But unlike dream-induced feelings, I don't dismiss these feelings because I sense that they derive from a source that transcends the human.

Rooftop Garden

Atop Casa Papa Giovanni, a retreat center in Assisi, is a small rooftop garden that overlooks the valley of Spoleto. I know this garden well, by day and by night, for one evening years ago I was locked out of the casa and spent the whole night in the garden, overcome by stars. The garden is mine now, as happens when we surrender ourselves to something that otherwise would have been a cause of impatience or anger or fear. The garden was dark and cold in the night air, but by surrendering to my predicament, I knew for the first time the night sky of Assisi and how Saint Francis felt sleeping beneath the stars locked out of his father's house.

There are plants here in profusion. (I say "here" because this rooftop garden I have with me always. For to paraphrase Ernest Hemingway, if you are lucky enough to have lived in Assisi, then you take it with you wherever you go, for Assisi is a moveable feast.) As I was saying when I heard Hemingway's words, there are plants here, geraniums, zinnias, azaleas, roses. And there are trees. Four cypresses, a fig, a palm, four pines and a row of six linden trees. There are three small lawns here, too, one round and two rectangular. And best of all, Brother Wind blows up here when down below it is close and still. Here the bells of Assisi ring more clearly and your eyes turn naturally to the ever-changing sky. In early morning fog blankets the valley though the sky is clear, and in late afternoon clouds rumble with dry thunder over the now clear valley.

There is something of Paradise here high above the rattling of cars and mopeds, the clattering of voices through the cobbled streets with their stone walls making the lanes of Assisi loud echo chambers that can be deafening. Here it is quiet, except for the bells and an occasional single-engine plane.

It is no wonder Saint Francis sought out mountaintops for prayer and contemplation. All through Umbria there are Franciscan mountain hermitages a day's walk apart, for Francis, as he preached and witnessed to the gospel on the road, as it were, always climbed a mountain at twilight, as did his Savior who, the Gospels say, went up the mountain to pray.

Dissociation

Prayer in the Franciscan tradition derives from the radical decisions made in living the gospel. A poor, wandering, preaching brother of penance is confronted almost daily with the poor, wandering, crucified face of Christ in those he meets along the way. How to respond to these faces? Only the gospel will show me. And not just reading the gospel, but meditating on the events of Christ's earthly life, placing myself there, drawing sustenance from the story, its power anointing my prayer only if I act upon the story's direction. Prayer and active charity, therefore, are complementary for the Franciscan. I pray to find the gospel way, I pray to live it, I pray I'll see it in the lives of those around me and I pray I'll respond as Jesus would.

Franciscan contemplation is never for me alone. It necessarily leads to the embrace and continuing support of the leper. No amount of crossed legs, open palms, silence, solitude or breathing deeply will do for a Franciscan's prayer life what embracing and trying to love someone I find it hard to love will do. I am brought to prayer again and again by the gospel imperatives uttered and lived by Christ and now challenging me in everyone I meet. Charity is impossible without prayer, and prayer is irrelevant without charity. Irrelevant because it is self-serving and illusory to attempt union with God without first attempting to love one's enemy. In one sense one's "enemy" *is* God and God is one's "enemy," for both are reluctant to talk to you and both take a lot of loving and giving of oneself before the conversation is easy.

Jesus himself is the measure of how much the love of God and neighbor exacts before one rises to new life, one with God and one's neighbor. Francis, too, is a measure, dying at age forty-five, almost blind, tubercular, malnourished, hemorrhaging with the wounds of the Christ he has meditated on and embraced in Christ's broken members. This is not the contemplation that moves beyond images; this is the contemplation of the images one becomes in living the gospel, in following, as Francis admonishes his brothers, in the footsteps of Christ.

Now, given this scenario or image of the Franciscan at prayer, is there any room for crossed legs, open palms, silence, solitude or breathing deeply? Saint Clare believed there is, so long as this contemplation, too, reaches out to those who minister on the road, as well as to those they minister to. For Clare and her sisters, all contemplating, cross-legged, open-palmed or not, was before the mirror of the Crucified Christ—mirror of the prayer and everyone the prayer must include to make of God the "enemy" turned lover and friend. Always that image for the Franciscan, the Crucified Christ. And if one should move to a prayer without images, it is *through* the image of the Crucified befriended that the gift of imageless prayer is granted. All is gift of the Crucified Christ. In him prayer is made as real as the hard love of loving one's enemy.

In what sense am I using "enemy" here in reference to God? God of course is not the enemy; God is "enemy" to my attempt to love and communicate and seek union with God without first loving my neighbor. God is "enemy" to the shortcut that bypasses God's creatures, that fails to come to God the way God first came to us—by descending into humanity, by incarnation of those spiritual aspirations that would deny or try to fly to God without the humanity made holy by Jesus Christ. God is "enemy" to that curious dissociation of prayer and charity that is sometimes evident in those who would live a life of prayer.

Portable Prayer

I came to Assisi to find Francis and Clare again, and so I do. But in Spello, the next town on the railroad run to Rome, I re-find their contemplative vision through the eyes of the Little Brother of Spello, Carlo Caretto. Fratel Carlo, as he was affectionately called, died in 1988, but his contemplative eyes and ears live on in his little brothers and sisters and in the many pilgrims who come to Spello to pray.

One of these little sisters, who calls herself a contemplative pilgrim, is Giovanna Negrotto. She lived and worked with Fratel Carlo during the last eight years of his life and now continues his legacy of leading pilgrims into hermitages of silence and contemplation throughout Italy's Umbrian Valley and beyond. In my conversations with her I learn much about prayer. I learn a new name for it, "contemplative pilgrimage," and I learn a way of beginning to pray as a contemplative pilgrim.

When Sister Giovanna is beginning a silent pilgrimage retreat with the pilgrims who have come to her to learn to pray, she welcomes them and gets them settled in their hermitage and then explains what their schedule there will be like, the practicalities of living in hermitage and the hours of common prayer. Then they eat a festive meal, conversing and introducing themselves to one another, after which Sister Giovanna begins to lead the aspiring hermits into silence and prayer. She is helped hugely by the staggering beauty of the valley below the hermitages of Spello, a small town between Assisi and Spoleto in the Umbrian valley.

The pilgrims are led outside and asked to sit and look out over the patchwork of farms below. Sister Giovanna then asks them to be silent and cover their eyes with their palms, their ears with their thumbs and listen to their breathing, becoming aware that there is Someone breathing within them. When they have done this for a few moments, she asks them to unstop their ears and listen to the symphony of sounds around them: the birds, the murmur of voices in the village below, the whir of traffic and blaring of horns in the distance.

"Imagine you are God's ears now," she says. "Listen with God's ears." This exercise is more prolonged than the initial covering of the eyes and ears. "Now drop your palms and open your eyes and see with the eyes of the One who breathes within you."

What this exercise does is to focus the attention, moving from the mind to the space within. There the prayer makes a space for God, a place of listening in silence, responding in love. This place within is where the prayer utters love-words to God. Here you are aware that you are a pilgrim wherever you are and that your pilgrimage is anointed, given meaning, by contemplating the world with God's eyes and ears.

What is important is to move out of the analytic mind, which distances things around you and adds to your anxiety by making you aware of chronological time and of how you are "wasting" time, by taking time to be out of time. Fratel Carlo used to expose the Blessed Sacrament in the monstrance and ask those who would to learn to pray to sit in silence for two hours before the Blessed Sacrament. Usually they were, to say the least, nonplussed. And he would then explain, "Imagine you are lying on the beach, thinking of nothing in particular, just letting the sun's rays work gradually on your skin, a beautiful tan emerging day by day. The host in the monstrance is the sun. Just be in its presence, not worrying about so-called distractions or whether or not you are concentrating on the 'sun.' A change gradually takes place in you the way a suntan emerges on the skin. Relax, let the 'sun' do its work. Your work is to *be* there."

Once, many years ago, I attended Sunday Mass at Spello. Fratel Carlo was sitting to the side, wearing the brown khaki shirt and pants he always wore. Many young people had been sitting in silence for two hours already. Then, as the priests rose and vested, singing, such as I'd not heard for a long time, broke the silence so gradually, so sweetly, it was like the hum of angels growing to a crescendo of praise and exultation. Out of what depths of silent adoration had this singing emerged? I was transfixed that such singing could anoint the air.

That image remains fixed in my mind. In all of us is potential for depth and joy if only someone would teach us to pray.

Healing Touch

I am sitting in your dormitory, Saint Clare, here on the second floor of the Church of San Damiano outside the walls of Assisi. Here you lived bedridden for many years; here you died. Here is a place of healing.

I bring to you here those who have asked me to pray for them. I lay them on the plain stone floor where you died, and I let you touch their brokenness, their illness, their pain, your hand tracing the sign of the cross on their forehead. I pray in silence as you minister to them. I simply hold in my heart the image of you blessing these broken ones.

It is early morning in late August. There is the soft shuffle of pilgrims' feet crossing the length of the dormitory. I remember how it was the first time I knew your gift of healing. A young Italian mother and father had rushed their young son up the steps to your dormitory. The boy had been hit by a car. They were taking him to the hospital in Perugia. They stopped here first. They believed your touch would save their son, and so they laid him on the floor where you lay broken eight hundred years before. The parents then rushed on to Perugia; the boy was not expected to live. But he did, and they knew it was you who had begun the healing which the doctors continued and God completed.

Later, I saw your healing touch heal others of their troubled memories, of hatreds, addictions and broken hearts. Your hand is strong, Clare; your touch is soft upon the soul.

I am here after nine years' absence from this place I've carried with me every day since last I sat here asking you to intercede for me, as well as for those I brought to you that summer. I knew someday you would bring me back, and so you have, and so I kiss the stone where you rested your weary feet.

I lay these poems here in gratitude for everything you've been for me during this novena of years away from Assisi. These poems, in fact, are your gift to me during those years, now given back to you here where you first showed me your gift of healing.

Before I ascended the steep steps to your dormitory, Clare, I prayed in the choir where you once prayed. I tried to reach in and touch (but could not) the choir stall where your intercession cured Brother Stephen of his madness, telling him to go and sleep in the place where you usually prayed. I wanted to fall down and sleep the deep sleep of the spirit, but I could not reach the place of your praying.

I walked instead the steps of pilgrimage, the prayer of ascent, and fell down here on the stones of your mystical union with Christ, which you wrote of to Blessed Agnes of Prague.

The Letters of Clare to Agnes of Prague

And Clare takes up her pen.
    She dips it in black
        indelible liquid.

She draws the letters that form the words
    that name the way
        into the Bridal Chamber,

to the place of waiting
    for the soundless step
        that arrives without walking,

without opening or closing doors
    without movement
        except the movement of her heart,

the Bride, hearing no sound
    yet knowing he's there
        beyond the hearing.

He—the paradox—in whose embrace is union and
virginity, in whose touch is chastity sealed. The words
    flow
from her pen, her hand moving where her heart
    leads—
further into the room where He adorns her breast with
precious stones, pierces her ears with gems shimmering
like blossoms in springtime. His left arm circles her
waist, his right circles her head with a crown, golden

for holiness. It is the Crucified Christ who steals thus into her bedroom, with whom she merges as with her own image in the mirror that is the crucifix, the corpus like the mirror's bronze disk convex with desire.

Can she write what she sees?

It is herself she sees in Him
    whose embrace, though rough and poor
        as the unbleached wool she wears,

is as familiar as her own arms
    wrapped round her shivering body
        standing in the dormitory's frigid morning.

She writes:
    Gaze into that mirror each day
        until you see your own face within it.

That contemplation wherein Jesus' face
    becomes your own,
        adorns your whole body

with the flowers and garments
    that are all the virtues:
        At the border of the mirror

the swaddling clothes of poverty;
    at the surface, the laborer's tunic of humility;
        in the depth of the mirror

the nakedness of Love
    hanging from the wood of the cross,
        Love Who's become the mirror of those

who long to mount the cross with Him,
    who cry out,
        Draw me after You,

embrace me happily,
    kiss me
        with the happiest kiss of Your mouth.[1]

NOTES

[1] Murray Bodo, *Icarus in Assisi* (Assisi: Minerva Press, 2002), p. 48.

Closure

Some Masses are harder than others. The two I dreaded most are now in the past—if a Mass is ever in the past—the funeral Masses for my mother and father, both of whom died suddenly and unexpectedly seven years apart. Mother's was first; I never thought I'd get through it, but I did. All during the Mass I knew my mother was seeing me through. The same was true of Dad's funeral liturgy.

Both Masses are a blur—I thought they'd be vivid—because all my focus was on making the liturgy beautiful and staying on top of my feelings. It was only later in Assisi that I celebrated a Mass for them during which I let grief have its way and surrendered Mom and Dad to God.

It was the year after Dad died that I returned to Assisi. My arrival in Assisi coincided with the annual commemoration of the dead on the Sunday following the Feast of the Assumption of Mary. It was a beautiful August morning, the sun almost lifting the graves of Assisi's cemetery heavenward. I concelebrated Mass with Don Aldo Brunacci, the founder of Casa Papa Giovanni, the retreat house where I've lived and worked during my many summers in Assisi. The Mass was outside on the steps of the small cemetery chapel of the Assumption, and as we raised our hands to make the Sign of the Cross beginning the Mass, I realized that this was to be the liturgy which would finally surrender my mother and father to the goodness and mercy of the Most High, All Powerful, and All Good God, as Saint Francis addresses God in his Swan Song, *The Canticle of the Creatures.*

Directly in front of us was the communal tomb of the Franciscan Friars of Assisi. Inscribed on the stone facade are the words of the last stanza of *The Canticle of the Creatures,* *"Laudato si', mi Signore, per sora nostra morte corporale, da la quale nullu homo vivente po' skappare."* "Be praised, My Lord, through our Sister Bodily Death, whom no one can escape."

Above this brave inscription is a sandstone frieze of two angels cradling and transporting the body of Francis to heaven.

Inside the chapel the central seventeenth-century fresco in the semi-dome above the altar depicts Jesus about to lift his dying mother to carry her bodily to heaven. It is a reversed pietà, Mary resting gently in her son's arms as he rested in hers after the crucifixion. The two side panels are of an aged Saint Joseph holding the hand of Jesus, who is looking lovingly up to Joseph, and a Madonna and Child. All is here in frieze and fresco: the son holding the father's hand, the son on his mother's lap, the son holding his dying mother in his arms.

And so on a Sunday morning in August, amid a profusion of gladioli, mums, lilies, roses, geraniums, morning glories, azalea and cyclamen and begonia, the tears running down my cheeks as they did not when I celebrated the funeral Mass for Mother and Dad, I surrendered them to the welcoming arms of Jesus.

Afterward, as we left the cemetery with its flat-topped cypresses like half-masted flags of the heaven-reaching cypresses that line the road back to Porta San Giacomo, I knew I had just celebrated the Mass of my life, the Mass of surrender. To our right lay the valley of the Tescio River, a dry riverbed that runs wet and wild when it rains on the surrounding hillsides. Like the arroyo of my youth, the Rio Puerco of Gallup, and like the soul, the Tescio waits for rain.

God's Work

Prayer, like fly-fishing, is something to do, a repetitive act that anchors the soul. My father's fly-fishing was a practice, a skill, a mastery that did not fail him, even when everything else seemed to be collapsing, like his job and future during the Great Depression.

My mother's cooking was her fly-fishing. She could and would cook from morning till evening. Polenta and spaghetti with their sauces of the Italian Tyrol, trout and quail, venison and elk, duck and pheasant, all garnished with the light Northern sauces sparing on tomato, which is so extravagantly a part of Southern Italian cuisine. Gnocchi and canederli, the latter an Italian version of the knoedles just across the northern border in Austria.

Today when I retreat into prayer for even a couple of days, images of my mother cooking rise from my soul's keeping, as in these lines written shortly after my mother died.

> I see you last in memory
> standing in light
>   watching your four rattling burners.
> The dense kitchen smells of garlic and sage
> heavy yet light
>   like your hand
> firm but delicate on the spoon
>   stirring, stirring,
> thick polenta
>   hardening into a cake.
> Quail sizzle, your pressure cooker's spout
> quivers, your wrist cricks with age.
> The pockets of your flowered apron-jacket
> sag with spoons and forks that lift and turn
> zucchini and doves, polenta and venison
> singing in your pans.
>
> You spoon syllables to my lips.
> I wish you could taste my words.

Now, here in Assisi, it is impossible not to think of my mother with the aroma of the distinctive Umbrian cuisine filling the air and lingering on my tongue after *pranzo*, the midday meal. I think of Saint Francis' interminable fasting and wonder how he did it here, where the smells of food waft tantalizingly through the streets of the city. He lived, it's true, with the lepers on the plain below, the stench of rotting flesh and poor sanitation assaulting his nostrils, and he begged leftover food, unappetizing in the hospital-like ambience of the leper colony. But he took his beggar's bowl into the city where quail *al forno* anointed the air. He must have thought of his mother's kitchen, as I do here, where the food is so like what she cooked and served all the days of my youth.

The sense of smell, they say, is strongest of the senses, triggering both memory and desire. Perhaps that is why Francis fasted so—for fear of turning his hand from the plow of God's field and returning to his mother's table. Perhaps he feared turning from serving to being served, from being one of the poor and outcast to being again the richest young man in Assisi. And so he fasted in order to smell another food, a heavenly food that seemed at first repulsive. As he wrote so beautifully in his *Testament*, "For I, being in sin, thought it bitter to look at lepers, and the Lord himself led me among them, and I worked mercy with them. And when I left their company, I realized that what had seemed bitter to me, had been turned into sweetness of soul and body."[1]

Francis did not fast because food was matter and not spirit and therefore somehow evil, as the Cathari believed. Rather, he fasted in solidarity with his Lady Poverty, whom he saw as the Bride of Christ, the only one who, when everyone else remained below, ascended the cross with Jesus. As in the songs of the troubadours, Lady Poverty became his Lady of the Castle, a metaphor and yet incarnate in the lepers and the poorest of the poor, who were for Francis the very image of the Poor Christ.

It is important to understand this dynamic of Saint Francis' thinking, lest we project our modern attitudes onto the Middle Ages and see Saint Francis as a masochistic, rather neurotic man.

Of the times of Saint Francis and the troubadour tradition, Joseph Campbell writes,

> [T]he mad disciplines to which a lover might, in the name of love, subject himself, sometimes approached the lunacies of the penitential grove.
>
> There is an account of one who bought a leper's gown, bowl, and clapper from some afflicted wretch and, having mutilated a finger, sat amidst a company of the sick and maimed before his lady's door, to await her alms. The poet Peire Vidal (c. 1150–c. 1210?), in honor of a lady named La Loba, "The She-Wolf," had himself sewn into the skin of a wolf, and then, provoking a shepherd's dogs, ran before them until pulled down, nearly dead—after which the countess and her husband, laughing together, had him doctored until well. Sir Lancelot leapt from Guinevere's high window and ran lunatic in the woods for months, clad only in his shirt. Tristan too went mad. Such lovers, known as Gallois, seem to have been, if not common, at least not rare, in the days when knighthood was in flower. There were some who undertook the discipline called in India the "reversed seasons," where the penitent, as the year became warmer, piled on more and more clothing until by midsummer he was an Eskimo, and, as the season cooled, peeled away, until in midwinter he was, like Lancelot, in his shirt. One is reminded of the childlike contemporary of these poets, Saint Francis (1182–1226), who conceiving of himself as the troubadour of Dame Poverty, begged alms with the lepers, wandered in hair shirt through the winter woods, wrote poems to the elements, and preached sermons to the birds.[2]

And so here in Assisi, wishing to be mad with love as Saint Francis was, at times I fast with Lady Poverty; at times I eat with my mother, celebrating the food she so lovingly prepared for me and Dad, the food that was her prayer, her charity, her selflessness. "The greatest treason," T. S. Eliot writes in *Murder in the Cathedral*, "is to do the right deed for the wrong reason." To fast out of fear of matter or of the body or of divine punishment is flawed; to fast in solidarity with the Lady Poverty, the Bride of Christ, is close to virtue; to fast when appropriate and to celebrate the gift of food when appropriate, is virtue.

I remember well our novice master scolding some of us one day for choosing to fast at table when Brother Francis, our cook, had taken pains to prepare an extra special meal. Not only had we failed in charity to one of our brothers, we had put our self-willed, misdirected "penance" above common sense; we had failed to respond with reverence to what was there before us. There is a time for fasting and a time for celebrating; we were only calling attention to ourselves, as the young are wont to do in their enthusiasm to excel in what they aspire to.

As we grow in the interior life and in understanding of God's working in our souls, we concentrate less and less on spiritual discipline as something we do, and more and more on spiritual discipline as something God does in us. Ours is only to make a clearing within for the God who wants to dwell within us. As Saint Francis says in Chapter 22 of the *Rule of 1221*, "We should make a dwelling-place within ourselves where he can stay, he who is the Lord God Almighty, Father, Son, and Holy Spirit." All our work is keeping that place for God; God will do the rest. And how we keep that place within, Saint Francis shows us in his *Letter to All the Faithful.* "We are his spouses when our faithful souls are wed to Jesus Christ by the Holy Spirit. We are his brothers and sisters when we do the will of his Father in heaven (Matthew 12:50), and we are mothers to him when we enthrone him in our hearts and souls by love with a pure and sincere conscience, and give him birth by doing good."[3] Everything else follows from this, whether we are cooking or fishing, eating or fasting, praying or celebrating with friends. God's work in us is centered in the place we've cleared within; our work is to respond to that work in faith, hope and, above all, charity.

NOTES

[1] Murray Bodo, *Through the Year with Francis of Assisi*, p. 82.
[2] Joseph Campbell, *The Masks of God, Creative Mythology* (New York: Penguin Books, 1976), pp. 175–176.
[3] Author's translation.

Meditative Prayer

The Franciscan vocation begins with a clean, dramatic break with the root of all evil—the love of money. The young, rich playboy, Francesco Bernardone, gives up all his earthly possessions and even his right to his paternal inheritance and embarks upon a lifelong pursuit of a life of evangelical poverty, chastity and obedience. "The Rule and life of the Lesser Brothers is this," he writes in his Rule of Life, "to observe the holy gospel of our Lord Jesus Christ by living in obedience, without anything of their own, and in chastity."

That initial radical break with *appropriatio*, the appropriation to oneself of what has been lent by God, the Great Almsgiver, is the beginning, middle and end of the Franciscan life. Without that break, prayer is a mere posturing; with that surrender of *appropriatio*, all prayer becomes possible.

It is obvious, then, that defining *appropriatio* and its refusal is the key to Franciscan prayer. The Latin word *appropriatio*, as Saint Francis uses it, embraces not just material things but spiritual realities as well. To appropriate as one's own: talent, virtue, health, money, possessions, reputation, fame, success and so on is to submit to Satan, the Father of Lies, whose basic sin is to aspire to divinity though he is a mere creature. I am a creature, and everything I am and everything I do and acquire belongs ultimately to "the Most High, All Powerful, Good Lord"—the words with which Saint Francis begins his *Canticle of the Creatures*. Therefore, acknowledging the infinite gap between Creator and creature is the beginning of the truth about oneself and the universe in relation to the Creator. The refusal to appropriate to yourself what is not yours is the beginning of humility, a virtue which is simply the truth about what is. How liberating is such a relinquishing of the illusion of "my." My things, my life, my reputation, my world, my, my, my. The relinquishing of *appropriatio* is the first step toward "we," toward communion with God and all God's creation.

Such an act of surrender leads to gratitude and praise, which is where prayer begins. I am not the source of my own being; all is gift. For Saint Francis, all is more than gift; it is a love-alms lent to me that I in turn may give it away, loving being diffusive of itself. As the dying priest says in Georges Bernanos's *Diary of a Country Priest,* "Everything is grace," everything is freely given.

Prayer, then, is simply the motion of the soul toward its center where the truth of the Creator/creature relationship is embraced and acknowledged, and where the relinquishing of a creeping *appropriatio* can again take place. In other words, life itself seduces and distracts us from the truth of who we really are, and we need—in order to remain human—to retreat from time to time for as long as it takes to encounter our own deepest truth: God within us and around us, before us and with us for all eternity, and our own need to adore, praise, thank and love the ultimate Source of our being.

Sometimes this movement of the soul requires a physical movement, as well, a retiring from the hustle and bustle of one's daily life. It is the way of the saint and the artist: retreat in order to see what is already there.

The more beset one is by external concerns, the more is the need to retreat wherever you are, even in the midst of your day-to-day living. For there is always some nook, some corner, park or quiet garden (even in your own yard) that you can move to in order to find the silence and solitude necessary to move into interior quiet.

From the time I was eleven or twelve years old, I have been able to find places conducive to prayer almost anywhere—at least for shorter periods of time like a half-day or day, or even a weekend. For longer periods one requires a place that will assure silence and solitude. And that is why Saint Francis retreated from the open roads to mountain caves when he wanted to enter more deeply into prayer. But if the place becomes more important than what happens there, the place itself becomes an obstacle to the movement of the soul, the movement of the heart.

I am writing these lines on a park bench next to a lagoon. A freight train blasts through the morning quiet, but not into my peace. The train is part of the peace, a reminder of the trains of my childhood—a welcome sound. I am here because the coffee shop I dropped into for a morning coffee was filled with crescendoes of chatter and busyness—unwelcome sounds. A dove coos, and I descend more deeply into the soul's center—"the sound of the turtle dove in the land"—all those biblical suggestions, those cadences that massage the soul for receptiveness. Something rises from within me to greet me. Is it you, Lord? Or something you've put there to remind me of you? Something like grace or peace or just some human aspiration?

Two sparrows punctuate the grass. Another dove echoes the first's coo. I close my eyes in expectation. The Feast of Pentecost is five days hence; my portable prayer is preparing my soul for fiery tongues.

When I open my eyes, sparrows hop soundlessly around me; the lagoon is silent as folded wings. None of this is mine, except the soul that welcomes it—and even that is not so much mine as me, and "me" belongs to God, the Creator, Redeemer, Sanctifier. I let go of *appropriatio,* and what I meant to relinquish returns as alms from God. I feel more me, and everything seems mine though I've just given it back to God.

The above very short scene contains the essence of meditative prayer, however long it may become in chronological time. For chronological time merely prepares for an experience that is outside of chronological time, the meeting of God with the soul. Such a meeting cannot be earned by putting in more time, but putting in time does prepare the soul's receptivity for what is essentially a movement of the Other from within the soul itself.

Hands

I look at my hands and see the hands of my father. I try to remember where and who he was when he was my age. I see the beginnings of my mother's arthritis in my two index fingers. I wonder how many others before them, grandparents and great-grandparents, these hands reveal.

The palms of my hands, unlike my father's, are soft, the hands of an intellectual, the hands of a priest. My father's hands mined coal and silver, quartz and gold. They boxed. They shot rifles, pistols, shotguns. They carried M-1s and mortar guns in World War II. They held the reins of horses and butchered cattle, deer and elk. They gutted wild game and fish and held a fly rod for over seventy years.

My mother's hands made beds and cleaned rooms and toilets in mining town boarding houses. They worked the farm and were burned over coal and woodstoves and over mangles in the laundries where she worked. They cleaned peoples' houses, folded sheets and other bedding at J. C. Penney's for twenty-five years. They chopped wood and hauled coal into the house and ashes out of the house. They cooked for me and Dad, changed my diapers and bathed me. They kept me safe; they rocked me to sleep. They folded countless times in prayer. They held her ever-present rosary. They wore the wedding ring I now wear attached to the chain around my neck.

Our hands are the hands of those who raised us, formed us, gave us the genes that make our hands like theirs. We carry our parents with us everywhere we go. Our hands remind us of that. They become objects of contemplation and prayer leading us inward where we see our parents looking at us looking at our hands. Outwardly, we continue to contemplate our hands. The outward glance has become inward seeing. We give thanks for our parents. We thank them; we thank God who gave them to us. Contemplation has led to prayer of thanksgiving, which leads in turn to prayer of praise. "Be praised, my Lord, you who have given me these parents who have given me these hands."

Still in the Mystery

I return to this rug, this chair where mystery sits with me. I almost touch my mother, my father, almost touch the mystery they inhabit as surely as I inhabit this space separated from the flying geese by this window and more completely by my otherness from them. I look up, and they are no longer there, but they are somewhere I can almost see, just as I am here beyond their seeing and knowing.

Sitting here makes me think such thoughts. Why I choose this rug has to do with my mother's importance to me. What you choose will be different, will be yours. But if you choose well, the object itself will be conducive to summoning up the unreachable whose mystery comforts and reassures a passage (ultimately) into the mystery of the eternal.

The allure of that almost contact, like the allure of your almost understanding what is being said here, is what keeps us returning to the mystery of prayer. We sit in the mystery in anticipation of the almost-experience that presages a space we will one day enter like Alice into and through the looking glass. We sit in the mystery as before a mirror that reaches back to us for that we look into it for—to see if we're still there. Only mystery's mirror is more: it reflects but lives apart, as well, its faces more than those that pass in front of it. It looks back with other eyes beyond and within your own eyes seen in its mere surface. Mystery's mirror is window, too, depending on where and how you look into it.

Learning to sit in the mystery helps us, therefore, to see ourselves, but also to almost see beyond ourselves. It helps us to both see and be seen in a new way that is an almost guarantee that we, too, will live beyond what we can now see and hear. Almost, because faith sits with us in the mystery. Faith, which is the almost, until we enter the mirror of eternity, and the final touch is real and forever.